Peter Ball lives in Wiltshire. After thirty years' ministry in parishes in London and as Canon Chancellor of St Paul's Cathedral, he enjoys an active retirement with an extensive ministry as a spiritual director. His earlier books on the adult catechumenate and on the Anglican tradition of spiritual direction reveal his strong interest in accompanying people on their journey of faith. Peter, married to Angela, has three children and nine grandchildren.

Introducing Spiritual Direction

Peter Ball

First published in Great Britain in 2003 by
Society for Promoting Christian Knowledge
Holy Trinity Church
Marylebone Road
London NW1 4DU

British Library Cataloguing-in-Publication Data
A catalogue record for this book is available from the
British Library

ISBN 0-281-05518-1

1 3 5 7 9 10 8 6 4 2

Typeset by FiSH Books, London
Printed in Great Britain by
Bookmarque Ltd, Croydon, Surrey

In grateful remembrance

of

Charles Preston, SSF
priest

and

Mark Hodson
bishop

Contents

Acknowledgements

The two haiku poems on p. 98 are copyright © St Mary's Abbey, West Malling, Kent, and are reproduced here by permission.

Material on the Myers–Briggs Personality Type Indicator and the enneagram in the Resources chapter is taken from a previous publication of mine: *Journey into Truth: Spiritual Direction in the Anglican Tradition*, published by Continuum/Mowbray in 1995.

By way of introduction

Who the book is for

In this book I am writing primarily for people who have heard about spiritual direction, are wondering what it means and whether there might be something in it for them – people who want to find out more about it. My first aim is to answer the questions that I expect these enquirers will be asking.

A second group I hope may be interested in reading the book consists of people who are already engaged in spiritual direction in one way or another. I am thinking here of those who regularly accompany someone else on his or her journey as well as those who are being accompanied. Third, there is a very important group of readers in the men and women who are taking part in training courses to prepare for exercising this ministry.

So I expect a certain seriousness of intent in my readership. Nothing over-solemn, let alone dull, but people who are in their own way committed to their search for something important in their life, their quest for meaning and truth and a desire for moving forward, for growth and discovery.

The practice of spiritual direction has grown remarkably over the past 30 years. Before then it was a fairly hidden ministry used by a relatively small number of people. Today it is better known across many of the churches. There are training courses in many locations across the UK for people who recognize a call to be spiritual directors, and many books have been written about it. But it is not yet part of the general knowledge of the Church and certainly not something that is on offer in the great majority of churches. In this book I hope to raise an awareness of what happens in direction and of the kinds of people who use it and how they are helped by it.

Sources

Two main resources underlie the book. One is the large number of talks I have had with upwards of 30 people who regularly use a spiritual director. Much of the book consists of lightly edited quotations from their interviews and I am extremely grateful to them for their time, their interest and their insights. Most passages within quotation marks are drawn from these conversations. The second resource is my own experience. Over the years I have been accompanied by four different directors. Their holy wisdom has been of huge value and I am sure that my own practice as a director has been greatly influenced by what I have learnt from them. Another source of learning has been the actual process of listening to people and the privilege of being invited to share in their lives. The activity, process, ministry – what is the right word? – that this book describes brings rich gifts to both participants, as I hope will emerge as you read on.

My story

A friend of a friend who was consulted about this book in the early stages replied, 'I suppose I would want a book like that to help me understand what it was like to be in a relationship of direction, both for the director and for the subjects. One would want an experienced director to be able to reflect accessibly on the way that his methods, approach and personal spiritual insight had developed in the course of time. Then I suppose it would be important to hear about the resources that nourish the director. It must be a truly pelican exercise at times, and the director runs the risk of being depleted by the whole activity.'

My own beliefs about spiritual direction will probably be obvious to any sensitive reader. Indeed in several instances I have made them quite clear. However, it is only right that readers should know something of the author's own story. So I lay my cards on the table; not that I claim in any sense to have all the answers, or even to know all the questions.

I feel a sense of recognition and deep gratitude. As I look at my own story and realize how much I have been given, I am yet again made aware of how much of this work is, in fact, gift and grace. Then, as I stress at several points through the book, spiritual direction is about a relationship – in God certainly – between two ordinary human beings.

To begin with, my basic belief is that spiritual direction is a relationship between two people that takes place within the presence of God. It has a sacramental nature, in that God uses the meeting as a channel for grace. Reginald Somerset Ward, the great Anglican director of the first half of the twentieth century, wrote to a friend:

3

There stands in my mind the experience I share with many other priests, an experience so constant and so proved that I cannot doubt it. It is the experience of being enabled, quite without my own volition, to see the need of a penitent or the exact knot at the centre of their difficulties. This experience leads me to believe that in spite of the worthlessness of the instrument God does use spiritual direction to help men and women to find and follow Him.

On the human side it calls for a willingness to be available, for a strong sense of trust and confidentiality, and for an openness and honesty on both sides. Ward wrote:

It would seem that the task of the spiritual director in the Church of England is not that he should be a judge or a dictator issuing commands, but that he should be a physician of the soul whose main work is to diagnose the ills of the soul and the hindrances to its contact with God; and to find, as far as he is given grace, a cure for them.

For me the most telling image is that of the companion on a journey. The journey is one of movement and growth towards maturity according to the pattern of Christ, and it involves a deepening of faith and a wholeness of personal response. Of course the journey is likely to pass through some passages of special difficulty or pain, and spiritual direction has its part to play is helping a person to work through these.

My own experience of spiritual direction, as with many of my generation, began with the practice of regular confession. Later the element of direction took on an increasing importance, though without eclipsing the sacrament of absolution. I have always seen my ministry of being a director for others as an aspect of my vocation and ministry as a priest. I was attracted to ordination in the first place because of a lively interest in people and I find it hard to think of anyone, lay or ordained, being able to work as a director without that. Although as priest I find that the sacrament of reconciliation, confession and absolution, in one form or another, often constitutes part of my meetings with people, I am increasingly aware that the direction relationship is in itself a means of grace.

A handful of people began to use me when I had been ordained for about eight years and was a parish priest, first in Wembley and later in Shepperton, but it was only when I was working at St Paul's Cathedral as a Canon Residentiary that the numbers grew. Spiritual direction formed an increasing part of my work once I left the cathedral for an independent ministry, and it is now a major part of an active retirement.

Resources

Training is something I feel rather ambivalent about. A large part of whatever ability I have comes, I am sure, from the experience of being directed by fine priests with a great deal of experience. I have learned by example. There have also been some elements of teaching – Reginald Somerset

Ward's *Guide for Spiritual Directors,* for example. Some years of following the 'Clinical Theology' course in the 1960s gave me an insight into human personality and behaviour that has been invaluable. For several years I was greatly helped as a director by supervision from Sr Elizabeth Smyth, who also recommended the internship in spiritual direction at the Jesuit Renewal Centre in Milford, Ohio, which I took in 1990. All of these have helped to raise my awareness of different aspects of the ministry and, I believe, have deepened my ability to do the work with people. However, perhaps more important than any training or example is the hidden effect of two things: a practice of regular prayer – the habit of being available to God – and also of listening to the people who come to talk with me – being available to men and women – have both shaped my ministry. Good directors are men and women who make a point of being there for God in their own spiritual life and who have a gift, which may indeed be honed by training and practice, of listening creatively to others. These are attributes that are hard to describe or define, but I believe that they are the essential prerequisites of the ministry. People who have them will find that others are intuitively drawn to them, whether or not they actually describe themselves as directors.

Concerns

With all the strong positive beliefs that I hold about spiritual direction, I also have some anxieties about contemporary trends. I see spiritual direction primarily as a vocation and a ministry and resist any move towards professionalization. I should be unhappy with any system of qualification or accreditation, and I suspect that I would be in the good company of most of those who run training courses in direction across the UK. I think there are problems too in the way that spiritual direction is regarded by some in positions of authority within the Church almost as a sentence to probation for clergy or ordinands who have run into personal problems. For all that it may in fact be effective, if those responsible suggest that 'a spot of spiritual direction will put the situation right or perhaps sort him or her out', this is a distortion of the true nature of the ministry.

Helpers in society

The roots of spiritual direction go deep, stretching back over the centuries in the writings and memories of past men and women. Through the Middle Ages and back to the Desert Fathers and Mothers of the early Church there are stories of holy companions, guides and teachers. The past few decades have seen a flourishing new growth in the practice, but spiritual direction is by no means the only player in the field. There are hundreds of different experts and agencies offering help and guidance to people, and it has become increasingly acceptable for people to seek help.

Think of all the different skills and insights that have come from the understanding of human psychology. Help is offered to people in personal pain according to a wide range of theories by psychotherapists, analysts and counsellors and with varying levels of intensity. There is help for those suffering from addictions in the various 'twelve-step' programmes stemming from Alcoholics Anonymous and now covering problems with drugs and gambling, among many others.

In business there are work consultants, trainers in leadership and personal relations. More generally, people look for help from life-coaches and all sorts of 'gurus'. Some gurus will in fact come from an Indian or other Eastern religion, though the word is often used simply to describe a wise and experienced personal guide. You can go on to think of all the facets of the 'body, mind and spirit' world that offer an eclectic mix of Eastern and Western spiritual and physical practice, moving some-times into the realms of astrology or the occult.

Nor should we forget the wide range of types of accompanying offered by social workers, doctors in general practice, health visitors and nurses, as well as people in charitable societies such as those concerned with people suffering from degenerative illnesses and their carers.

Clearly spiritual direction shares many of the goals and some of the skills and approaches of many of these others in the helping field. I hope this book will serve to give people the information they need as they choose whether spiritual direction is the course for them.

Terminology

Before going much further we need to cope with the difficulty of the name itself. 'Spiritual direction' is what most people call this relationship. As a title it is by no means an ideal, but it is the one most commonly applied and so I shall continue to use it. It has a long history going back for centuries to describe the relationship in which a more experienced Christian offers to help another to learn and grow in the way of faith and life. But the words carry all sorts of overtones that may cause problems.

'Spiritual' can give the impression that it is concerned primarily, or even exclusively, with spirituality, a person's prayer life or mystical experiences. In actual practice the conversation between a person and a director covers life in all its many aspects. The spiritual side certainly plays an important part but is by no means the only aspect. Rather, spiritual direction is about the whole person and the whole of life, with its mix of relationships and events, hopes and fears, work and leisure – indeed the whole intimate connection between all that a person is and does and his or her spiritual nature. Spiritual direction is concerned with helping people make sense of things, of God and of the depths of the spirit, all taking place in the context of a human being in the real world that we inhabit.

There are problems with the word 'direction' too. It sounds directive, as though the relationship could be one in which the director tells you what to do and how to live. If you put 'spiritual' in there as well, it could give the impression that the point of it was to have a director who would tell you how to live the spiritual life. We shall see, as we go through the book, that it is more likely that a director will reflect, encourage, suggest, even guide perhaps, but only very occasionally give firm advice on how a person should behave.

As someone said to me, 'There is the snag about what to call it. "Spiritual direction" sounds as if it's being told what to do, rather that you coming to say what's on your mind, on your heart and going away feeling, perhaps, "Well, it's better than I thought it was" or, perhaps, "This is something I need to deal with." It's about encouragement.'

One name for the ministry is the phrase in the Anglican Book of Common Prayer, 'ghostly [spiritual] counsel'. The idea of spiritual counsel suggests advising, but it also carries echoes of the practice of counselling. As we shall see later, counselling has its own purposes and methods and is different from spiritual direction.

The name 'soul friend' is sometimes used to describe a spiritual director. It looks back to the old Celtic use describing the relationship and became popular following the publication of Kenneth Leech's book with that title, *Soul Friend: A Study in Spirituality*.

There is also the question of what word to use to describe the men and women who come for the help of a spiritual director. The trend of the past decades to describe people as 'customers' rather than as patients or passengers has no place here. I am concerned to emphasize the independent responsibility and personal autonomy of the person seeking spiritual direction. This means that I am wary of describing these people in a way that overemphasizes the director's role in their life. Quite a few people talk about 'directees', but that is a word which jars with me. I feel it is too passive and also somehow demeaning; it seems to define the person primarily by his or her relationship with the director, whereas I am concerned to emphasize the value of each person in his or her own right. The word 'client' is less passive, since it indicates that the person has come asking for something, but it carries strong echoes from social work or therapeutic counselling, which are not really appropriate here. Others talk about 'pilgrims', which certainly gives weight to the all-important idea of journey, but, to my mind, it tends to limit it to something specifically religious. A very experienced director used to speak simply of 'friends', which is simple, and I find I follow his example quite often, even if this is a special kind of friendship quite unlike most others.

Outline of this book

In the chapters that follow I first ask what sorts of needs, hopes or motivations cause people to look for a director. This is followed by hearing what people feel that they get from the ministry and what gifts they recognize in the process. Looking at the relationship itself, I review several aspects, practical and more personal, as well as considering some of the snags and difficulties that may arise. I also consider the similarities and differences between spiritual direction and counselling.

Hoping that after reading so far you may want to go further, I then suggest ways of finding and choosing a spiritual director. Two chapters follow on praying; the first is a general chapter about the various ways in which people pray, and the second focuses more sharply on the prayer of silence and contemplation, drawing heavily on an article I wrote for *Presence*, the journal of Spiritual Directors International.

The chapter on resources notes some of the needs felt by spiritual directors and ways to meet them. In suggesting a few books for further reading, I have chosen ones which I have personally found helpful.

What are you looking for?

A friend was speaking for many when she said, 'Lots of people think that spiritual direction is only for the clergy and people with positions and ministries in church, but they're wrong. It could and should be much more widely used. Even now that it is becoming trendy, it's still very limited.' The purpose of this chapter is to consider the kinds of people who ask for and use spiritual direction and to notice the reasons why they do so. We shall see that there is nothing frivolous about the people who turn to spiritual direction. Whatever the background from which they come and the reason that has prompted them, they are serious in their search.

Routes to direction

There is a very wide range of needs or situations that lead people to a spiritual director. What they have in common is that they are aware of a strong urge to go deeper, to take seriously their quest for meaning in life or to find help on the journey of faith in God.

Contemporary writers use different images to describe the way in which faith can mature from something that is received from one's parents or other early authority figures through to a faith that is fully accepted by a person and fully expressed in that person's life in relationship with others and society. Experience shows that, in a similar way, there are times along the journey of spiritual development when people are more likely to seek and benefit from spiritual direction than others. I suspect also that there are those who are simply not the kind of people who will ask for it. Along with others engaged in spiritual direction I have been made aware of two groups of people or perhaps a range of people's attitudes with two poles.

At one end, or in one group, are the people for whom faith is a matter of assent to statements. They are people for whom the content of belief matters a great deal. They tend to look to the authority of the church, to tradition and to leaders in their community for validation. Their beliefs and their attitudes tend to be black and white, often with an added sense of exclusivity. The faith community in which they feel at home may well have rather tight boundaries and a strong emphasis on conformity. If they work with a director, they may well look to her or him for expert advice or clear guidance on the choices they have to make.

Most of people who have come to me for direction are found in a second group of people who find their faith not so much in clearly defined answers but rather in being faithful to the quest for understanding. They find themselves in a situation where each question that is answered produces a further question to work at. They are people for whom their local faith community may well not be as satisfying as once it was. They do not feel at home with many of its attitudes and often complain that they no longer feel nourished by what their church offers. They are aware of and begin to feel at home with ambiguity and to respect differences between people. Increasingly they are able to trust their own experience and judgement. However there is often a sense of loss and of lostness when the old community values and certainties become weaker. Guilt can come in here too, with the feeling that they are letting down a whole range of people and beliefs that were once highly valued. It is for people who are in this sort of position that spiritual direction can be valuable. It gives them a non-judgemental relationship in which to explore what may feel like dangerous ground and, I hope, it is somewhere that they can recognize that they are accepted as normal and not weird or unusual, let alone wicked and worthy of condemnation.

When I listened to people talking about their experience of using direction, I was aware that very often they came to it at a time when there was some sort of change taking place in their life. Sometimes it was in their spiritual life, but more often in the circumstances of their ordinary life or work, or in their close relationships with other people – as one woman put it, 'It's a mixture of accompanying on the ordinary road, plus times of crisis and times for big decisions. I have nowhere else I could have dealt with the material we've worked on. I sometimes think my director knows me better than I know myself. I feel very supported; I know I can ring in a crisis and I trust her to tell me if I'm going badly astray.'

Spiritual changes

The spur to seek direction may be when something new happens in a person's spiritual life, when old patterns are disturbed. One friend described how, 'It all started with a vivid personal experience of the Holy Spirit. I went to my vicar to find out more about it; he was concerned for me and worried I might become all "happy clappy". He suggested that direction might help, and the course I was on at the time suggested it too. So I began. I needed it to explore what the experience was all about. Something had happened, which I would say was an encounter with God, and I didn't know how to describe it, what to do about it or what it meant. There were also changes in my prayer life. I needed someone to talk to.'

People recognize that things are changing for them and they feel it would be good to have someone else to help them test what is happening, as with another friend who said, 'I was first attracted by it because I realized I was at a growing stage in my journey. I needed to look at it with someone else, needed to evaluate where I was going and find someone to help in checking whether it was OK. There was a sense of exploring: it was more about questioning and less about definition. It was someone to help look at what was going on. Although I had close friends with whom I talked about the spiritual journey, now I needed someone a bit more objective.'

When people begin to look for a companion on their faith journey, it shows that they are taking it seriously. It may be that they want someone to be with them as they enter new and frightening territory, as with someone who said, 'When I began spiritual direction, I felt like an insect skating on the water. I sensed a desire to "go deeper", but I didn't really know what it meant. At the same time I was frightened of what going deeper would entail in terms of sacrifice of autonomy, money, comfort, or profound change of life. My director kindly, almost flatteringly, called it a desire for God; I have perhaps feared that it was a desire for an emotional wallow, perhaps a wish for what they used to call "consolations". How much weight should one give to feelings? How much can one trust them? For instance, last week at Mass, completely out of the blue, I was swept by a longing for God so strong I could almost touch it. It only lasted for the tiniest moment, but I wonder if that isn't enough. I think it probably is. Perhaps the longing for God is a great grace in itself.'

A friend who has been a faithful Christian for most of her life and recognizes that her way of being faithful has developed over the years described it like this. 'My experience of spiritual direction has been one of being accompanied in a deepening "yes" to God, entering more and more into unknowing, letting go of my "God-in-a-box theology" that was strangling the reality of God in my life. My director's encouragement has helped me increase my availability to God, grow as a person, learn to be gentle with myself, and come to a place of self-acceptance and love, which has enabled a deeper connection with others. I have had many "helpers" in my life, including three psychotherapists, but a spiritual director (especially one of 15 years' standing) is a companion as valuable to me as a riverbed is to a river, supporting the flow of my stream to the ocean which is God.'

The spur for some people may come through taking part in a particular religious event. It could be a retreat, a week of guided prayer in the local church, or the experience of a renewal of faith on a special weekend event such as Cursillo, as one regular churchgoer told me: 'It was after a retreat in the parish; I talked with the organizer, who suggested I find a spiritual director. I was looking for encouragement, number one, and I have found it. Somehow it brings the presence of God nearer. I feel God is in our meeting. I know that tomorrow morning I shall be able to pray.'

Church relationships and change

As I suggested earlier, spiritual direction can be extremely useful in helping people feel or think through their relationships with the church they belong to. Let me begin with the example of how over the years it has been a particular privilege to be invited to accompany a number of women on their often arduous journey towards ordination as priests. In some cases we have walked together for a period of years through their ministry as deaconess, deacon and priest. Not that any of their journeys was without pain. Through the time of waiting and uncertainty and the often vicious opposition that they encountered, they knew themselves to be called; and their call was so often affirmed by the congregations they served. Others have begun with me as committed lay members of their churches and later found their vocation to be ordained. Women ordinands today are spared those years of doubt.

A key moment was the time after the legislation went through when deacons were asked to write to their bishop saying why they believed they should be priests. The memory of the conversations as we talked though those letters remains vivid. Almost all found it hard to envisage what it could be like the other side of priesting, but all spoke in different ways of the gap they recognized in their ministry, caring for people in the parish at a deep level, yet unable to celebrate the Eucharist for them. Nearly ten years later I notice that it is the women priests who speak most often with joy and wonder at their experience of presiding at the sacrament.

A woman who has been many years in ministry spoke of the value of direction in her life. 'I particularly value the support I've received, especially over all the women priest business. My director was someone I could come to, have a cry with, be angry, say whatever I was feeling and know it was all right to be like that, because it really was serious stuff. He helped me to know it was OK to be where I was, in spite of the pain around it all, and helped me to go off and be joyful again. Looking back, though it wasn't why I began, that became very important. It's been a focus time when I could talk about how it was for me. Most of the time you've got to keep that locked up and get on with what you're there to do.'

Clergy in general are often encouraged to have a spiritual director, and a good many do so. A vicar in a suburban parish told his story, which shows the need for a director who understands the demands of a life in ministry and who is sympathetic to different traditions. 'Before I started with spiritual direction, I mostly dumped on my wife. For some time she'd had direction for herself. When there were difficulties in the parish, she was very supportive, but she also urged me to find a director. The title put me off for a while and then I also wanted a good evangelical who would know "where I came from". For three years I went to a senior priest, who wasn't actually trained as a director, and found it good. I was able to talk honestly, with gentle prompting on his part, about the priority of a relationship with God, and to see how central a relationship of love was. It was the start of facing up to the value of something like that and it led on to taking the spiritual direction course, which helped me to be honest and vulnerable with other people. Then that priest retired and moved. I might have dropped the idea but the course required me to have a director and made me realize the need to be more honest and vulnerable, to be open to the importance of self-awareness in the spiritual life – which is what it's about! I used to go to my old director just three times a year; that was not as good as double that frequency, which we have now. There wasn't the same sense of following through in an ongoing way.'

Life's situations and problems

Some people first seek out a spiritual director because they are finding it difficult to deal with events in their life or with the relationships in which they are involved. One woman described how, when she was working with dying people in hospital, she got very stressed. 'Our curate suggested that spiritual direction might help and I asked the person who was my guide in a special week of prayer to be my director. I am the only one on our team of lay ministers who has one. I find it's a good way to sort out your thoughts and worries; it helps deal with the jumble and put things in perspective.' Another spoke of how it was difficult at home. 'I couldn't talk to my husband, and the vicar suggested I needed to meet with someone who was outside the situation. He suggested a possible director and it was a relief to speak with someone who knew what I was about.'

External pressure

The motivation to find a spiritual director does not always come from within. There are pressures of different intensity which come from outside. It may just be that a friend whom you trust has suggested that the way of spiritual direction might help you, and a kind of loyalty urges you towards it. It may be that you have been recommended to find a director by someone in the church who is helping you consider a possible call to ministry. Men and women who are investigating a vocation to ordination or people who are joining the lay branch of a religious community as tertiaries or oblates are often strongly advised, if not actually required, to get themselves a director. This may be fine or it may cause real problems. An ordinand described how there were three groups on her course. There were the people who already had a director and found it useful. There were the people who had been strongly recommended to find one and who had discovered that they were being helped by the experience. And there was the third group of people who felt that they had been pressured into finding a director and resented the fact that it did not seem to work for them. One friend described a position somewhere between the last two. 'To be quite honest the main reason I started was because I was told I ought to. As part of our ordination training we were supposed to have someone to talk to. So I was not sure what I expected to get out of it. I suppose I was looking to be helped to understand myself better; to have help in deepening my relationship with God; and if there were any particular problems and difficulties, I'd have a sounding board, somebody to talk it over with. So what do I get out of it? It varies from time to time whether I come away feeling it's been helpful or not. I'm not sure how much I benefit from it. I had no idea what was expected, so I'm not sure whether I'm using the time properly. I suppose it does help me to be aware of what is happening. During the training for ordination there are all sorts of inputs; seeds are sown from all over and it is hard to know where all the growth comes from. And then I've not had any particular crises that have needed special help and I have a wife I can talk to, books I can read and two or three particular Christian friends to share with. Fellowship and sharing and talking about the Christian life is very much part of my tradition.'

Another friend described how she found herself in the second group. 'I started direction because of an obligation. Now I would want to continue it as an opportunity, rather than an ought. It makes you think things through for yourself. If problems arise, you've got someone else to talk it over with. It helps to clarify your own way of thinking. It is someone you can let your hair down with, who doesn't hold up her hands in horror at the things which happen. It was part of my rule when I joined the Franciscans as a tertiary to make regular confession. I began with the very helpful vicar until he retired. Then I found my present director many years ago and now couldn't live without it. I have to fill in forms to say when I've visited my director, with dates. But compulsion makes no difference to our relationship.'

Sometimes the way into spiritual direction goes in stages as other people make suggestions, as life's circumstances change or as one's spirituality develops. The wife of a priest told me, 'I remember our bishop said that clergy wives needed someone other than their husband to help sort out their spiritual life. It was when there was a Franciscan mission that I began formally with confession. I felt very unburdened and released; it was somewhere where I could speak my whole mind. I felt it was a kind of extension of a church service. But then as time went on I found I didn't feel the need for formal confession so much and we talked more informally. It is still a form of confession. It gets down to what is most important. Really what I am here for is to love God with all my heart and soul and mind and strength, and that's what I want to do and to find the way to do it, without my self and my own problems interfering. I find my director is able to point out what is a real sin and what is something that springs from my depressive nature.'

The wife of another priest, who is now herself ordained, told her own story of what different direction relationships had meant to her. 'When my husband was at theological college, students were encouraged to use spiritual direction and confession. I watched him and others go to this mysterious thing and come back and saw it made a real difference to them. I thought it was very scary, but decided I'd have a go. So I went a couple of times before we left and found it valuable enough to find someone else when we moved. I've had a director ever since the late 1980s. It began with both sacramental confession and spiritual direction as part of the same thing. I'd only been a Christian for two years. It was something about sorting out the difference between what you do feel guilty about but shouldn't, and what you should feel guilty about and ought to deal with. That was scary but valuable in getting rid of pointless guilt. Then after two years I met a lady who led a retreat in our parish and I went to her for direction. She was an experienced lay woman. It was still a matter of sorting out, but now more about sorting me out than sorting what I needed to feel guilty about. She was very encouraging of me. She was a very respected member of the church but also very left-wing, which suited me and encouraged me. Until then, being so new to it all, I'd been a very "good girl". She helped me to integrate some of the other side of myself and also to integrate the artist in me. She helped me realize things about myself which are difficult to talk about in respectable Christian terms! She moved away and two years without anyone was difficult. It took me a while to do something about it. Then I asked a nun I met and she suggested my present director.'

What are you looking for?

Everyone seems to recognize that spiritual direction is serious, important stuff and needs a relationship of trust and acceptance, as the following statements indicate.

'I was looking for someone to trust, someone I can say anything to. I don't want to feel I have to be careful. I want to know I can talk about God and my relationship with God at a very deep level. That doesn't become sanctimonious twaddle because it's real. What helps is the actual person. Nothing I say can make him raise his eyebrows. I can talk about anything; so trust is most important, and confidentiality.'

'Previously I had used informal directors, people to talk to about a specific question. The most daunting thing was how to find one; then what if you're put off? I guessed it would be space to talk and be supported by a director. I found I was very guarded at first; unsure how much of me I was willing to expose. I kept myself to myself. I found it hard to speak about faith. I was worried that I wasn't doing it correctly. I was at the stage of moving into a new way of faith and didn't want anyone to say I was up the wrong gum tree. I was very wary, which is not a good thing in direction. But I found that as the relationship matures, it becomes more comfortable. It wasn't comfortable at first.'

'What was I looking for? I had no sense of drifting from the faith. I recognized that God knows all. But I thought there would be value in getting a wise person who is not involved in any way to give an opinion. A wise, impartial friend with no axe to grind whatever; someone I didn't see for any other purpose and with whom I had no relationship for family or business, someone who would be positive and helpful. As for forgiveness, whether it was effective or not (I was doubtful about a priest's authority to forgive sins), there would be grace there. So I was looking for grace and outside advice. And that is what I have got from it. John Wesley writes in his diary about his conversion and his heart being strangely warmed. When he gets back to his house the tempter says, "This can't be love. Where is thy joy?" He suggests that God gives joy to some and to others not, according to the counsels of his will. The same is true of forgiveness; sometimes it is felt, sometimes not. Over 15 years I've drawn great strength from it and certainly wouldn't want to give it up. But equally I wouldn't want it to become mechanistic. Then it wouldn't seem like spiritual counsel and wouldn't help me.'

'I had had informal direction for years with encouragement from older Christians; then I took it up formally at college, when I realized my need for a companion on my journey. I suppose I've always benefited from an older, parent figure, a more experienced Christian to help me on the way. Now I see spiritual direction as an important part of my rule of life; it's a strand of my spirituality which needs to be there to keep it ticking over effectively.'

Clergy directing clergy

Several of the priests I spoke with told me that they felt it was specially helpful to have a director who was also ordained. One said, 'In looking for a director I am looking for companionship on the journey; someone a bit further on the way than me, with an understanding of where I'm at spiritually and as a priest. I need to distinguish what is personal and what is ministry; the two often pull in different directions. Direction is very personal; it's for me; not just about my ministry. It is very helpful for unloading the joys and sorrows of daily life, specially with a fellow priest; each understands the other's circumstances and the pressures you are under. You want to deepen and tune into your spirituality. You find that it makes insights available to you that you might not have yourself. A director can take more of a helicopter view. I welcome input, but it needs to be based on what the director has found valuable in his own journey. It's not so much a being told as a being shared with. Spiritual direction is not a "telling" situation. That was not how Christ worked. He worked with stories and questions and looked for a sign of faith to enable healing.'

The subject boundaries are very broad. 'It's about the whole of what's going on in my life, not just about what happens when I say, "Right, I'm going to say my prayers now". The whole, hopefully, is integrated. It's about how I respond to what's going on. Spiritual direction enables

me to reflect on life and where God is in that. It helps me
to let go of what needs to be let go. Often it's only in the
looking back that I can see where God is in it. It's
important not just to rush on to the next task; you need to
recognize God in the past and the present before finding
his way in the future.'

Spiritual direction and confession

There is a considerable discussion among people
concerned with spiritual direction over its relationship
with sacramental confession and absolution, or reconciliation as it is known by contemporary Roman Catholics.
One of the gifts of the Oxford Movement, the Catholic
revival in the Church of England, was the reintroduction
of confession as a live option in Anglican spirituality. The
sacrament was always provided for in the Book of
Common Prayer in the order for the Visitation of the Sick
and was recommended in the homily before Holy
Communion for people who were unable to quieten their
own consciences. It is now widely, if not universally,
accepted in the Anglican Church and many older church
people's experience of spiritual direction began with the
counsel given within a discipline of regular confession.

It is unlikely that anyone looking for direction now
would expect that it would necessarily include confession.
Partly this is because the constituency of those who see the
value of direction has widened far beyond the traditional
Anglo-Catholic wing of the Church, and partly it is
because there is now a wide variety of people offering

direction. Until fairly recently the vast majority were priests. Now with the increasing number of lay directors, both women and men, the ministries of listening and accompanying people and the offering of sacramental reconciliation have tended to move apart. However, it is worth noting the experience of three people for whom confession and absolution plays a part in their spiritual direction, as well as comments from those for whom it seems foreign.

A lay woman working in local government described how for her the balance between confession and spiritual direction had altered over time. 'I've had spiritual direction continually for the last 20 years. When I was a student considering a vocation to be a nun I was in touch with a Mirfield Father. I joined a religious community for a few years until I realized it was not for me and left. Then I took some time out. When I came back to church I found confession a help. Spiritual direction was part of that, rather than what I have come to now, which is primarily direction with confession sometimes as part of it. Now it's a lot broader, not just talking about all the things that have gone wrong. It's more thinking about the whole of my life and what God is saying to me, rather than looking at it and saying, "I'm a rotten sort of person; I've upset God in all these ways". I think it was probably a necessary stage. St Teresa says that when you start, there are all these ghastly things outside your castle which you have to get across. Once you're in the first room, you can still hear them gnashing away. So you have some ground clearance to do before you can actually start planting and growing.'

'I had six years with a lovely confessor who wouldn't have called himself a spiritual director. Then I needed something different and it so happened that he moved away at about that time. That's when I felt I wanted to talk about a lot more than just making my confession. In the old days there were lists of sins in confirmation books. What was the point? I find it's better in spiritual direction when it's not so formal; it's a relief and infinitely more helpful.'

'As a student I made my first confession to a friar at Cambridge, which helped at quite a difficult time I was going through. Then not for many years; I was a church-goer, but no confession or spiritual direction. When I was training for a lay ministry, I spoke with my bishop, who suggested I could be helped by spiritual direction and put me in touch with my present director.'

On the other side a friend said, 'I wonder whether there are things I wouldn't bring to my director. I am not sure about using him as a confessor; I don't think I would. It doesn't seem appropriate in the spiritual direction relationship, but I can't think why not. I might talk about it with him outside the direction session.' This observation was echoed by someone who put it like this: 'I've never made confession in spiritual direction, though I have once been to formal confession separately. I think it's linked with dealing with the shadow side: God's grace at work rather than our sin.'

Summary

When we speak about crisis intervention, the words carry an overtone of urgency, panic, even impending disaster. There are occasionally times when people seek spiritual direction in that sort of emergency situation and there are times when situations like that arise in an ongoing direction relationship, but they are not the norm. The root meaning of the word 'crisis' has to do with judgement, choice or decision. It is in that area that most people are looking when they approach a director. They are aware that it would help them to have another person sit with them as they look at their life, see what kinds of choices lie before them and discern what God's will may be for them at this particular point in their journey. There may not be any dramatic happenings to be faced or any major decisions to be made, but a person recognizes that the opportunity of spending time with a more experienced Christian and being heard will help in coming to terms with life, beginning to make sense of it, perhaps even seeing where God is in the events and relationships of life and in his or her attitude to these events and relationships.

Gifts

I find it a source of wonder that so much can grow from two people making a habit of meeting for about an hour for a certain kind of conversation regularly over a period of time. It sounds so simple and so ordinary, and in a sense it is. Two people make an arrangement to sit down together every so often. In a private room, with the assurance of the privacy of confidentiality, one person talks about whatever seems important and the other listens carefully, occasionally saying something to reflect what he or she has heard, perhaps asking a question to get some greater clarity about a point and sometimes responding with a comment. For that is the essence of spiritual direction, allied with the fact that it takes place against a background of a shared acceptance of faith or at least the importance of the journey of faith.

This chapter sets out the stall for spiritual direction, outlining what people have said they get out of inviting another person to share in their journey in this way. You can think of it as the kind of testimony from satisfied users that you find in some sorts of advertisements. There are several aspects of gifts that people value in those hours. There is the time itself, the sense of God's presence there and the reassurance that comes from being heard, and the support that is given by a director's trust and occasional advice. Then there are the ways in which people observe that these gifts are enabled. The chapter ends in a brief discussion of the relationship between spiritual direction and counselling.

Listening

The time and the listening provide a space where people can be free to be themselves, to be honest with themselves and with the director and to be free from pressure. It is very rare in life that you get the opportunity to be listened to properly, to be really heard. That is one of the most important things that spiritual direction offers and it is what most people are searching for when they look for a director. It is also one of the key points by which they judge whether a director is helpful or not. A good director is one who has the ability (and perhaps also the training) to be fully available to the other person. Listening means giving your full attention; it is active rather than passive and the listener has a vital part to play. A young clergyman used a telling image: 'Spiritual direction is not bouncing off a wall, it's not looking in a mirror (when you just see yourself); it's more like a painted portrait; a person interprets. That's really helpful. I need my own thoughts clarified.'

There is more to listening than just using ears. Obviously, if you want somebody to help you, you need the other person to understand where you are and what kind of problem or opportunity you are faced with. The other person needs to listen and you need to talk. But good listening has a deeper use than simply receiving information. Being heard implies many different things. It means that what you have to share has been shared, whether it is painful, exciting, scary or shaming. You have had the chance to get it off your chest and someone else is able to carry part of it with you. There is a release of pressure; you have off-loaded some of the weight. A friend described what it meant to her like this: 'It is important to me to feel heard. It is quite demeaning to be passed over. To have someone really listen to you means that they reckon you are worth listening to. Listening is a sign of respect and value. At a profound level it is a sign that you have worth, even that you are loved. It is acceptance, the opposite of rejection.'

A local government officer told me, 'It's good to have one person focused on you, because in today's life most people don't have that; someone detached but engaged with you. In the world and in society it is hard to be listened to. What I value is an hour when I know I have got his attention, the value of the listening. I think I've grown through being with someone of a different churchmanship who has been able to meet me where I am and understand the differences. If I'd had someone of my own charismatic evangelical tradition it would have been less creative or productive. Where else in life would you have another person there to listen to you for a whole hour? It sounds so self-centred, but it is intensely valuable.'

People may have close friends with whom they talk openly about things that matter deeply to them, but it is not usual to talk solidly for an hour about your own life. Friendship – politeness even – requires that you give the other person a chance to tell his or her story. But in spiritual direction the time is there for you. It is all yours. As one person said, 'My director has time for me, non-judgemental and understanding.'

God and the gospel

In the listening and the time and the space there is a clear recognition of the purpose and meaning of the meeting. It takes place with God. People often speak of being aware that it is not two but three people in the room. Often the room where you meet may have a symbol such as an icon or a cross in it. As someone remarked, 'I appreciate the fact of the candle, the blessing, the time and space.'

Myself, I come back very often to the words of an elderly Sister who said to me, 'Whenever I am due to meet with someone, I pray to the Holy Spirit to empty me of myself, so that I can listen only to Him and the other person.'

Two people spoke to me about how they saw the God-dimension in the meeting. A long-standing churchgoer said, 'Your spiritual director is a Christian who has a listening ear to God. When you come with lots of things crowding in, you can't listen to God. The relationship gives space. My director listens to what I say and sometimes points a direction that, maybe, I'd have gone on anyway but would have taken longer. In a world that increasingly ignores the Faith and knows nothing and cares less about the riches waiting to be had for the asking, it is an enormous help to look at one's life in the light of the gospel and thereby be reminded of what is really important.' And a younger person wondering whether she ought to change jobs said, 'Spiritual direction is a sounding board; saying my thoughts aloud earths them and helps me see what I should do next. When I say I don't know what to do next, I get a reaction from my director because she is a person, which I don't really get from God. She could be the God-person – God telling me. I find my own way by voicing the mess to her and sometimes she says nothing at all; sometimes positive suggestions and advice; sometimes just, "Um". She doesn't really have to say anything. I am the one who sorts out which way to go. When I've been to see her, it's up to me to take or leave any advice she may give.'

Life as lived

By now it will be clear that the relationships and events of ordinary life provide most of the material for the conversation in a spiritual direction session. 'What I really appreciate is the space. Someone who can listen to me witter on about what's going on in my life. Because what is going on in my life is so involved with the spiritual that I don't actually separate them out. A good director is someone who has the patience to realize that when I am wittering on about things that seem very concrete in my life, it's bound up with the spiritual. So the whole lot's important and I need to have someone who can take that on board. Someone I can really trust; that means a person who is really listening, who's really open about what's going on in my experience, who hasn't got their own agenda to push, who's not going to be judgemental, who will accept my experience as valid, but who will also look at it with me objectively and, if need be, challenge me on it.'

A young priest described the gift like this: 'It's like writing a journal; it helps to make sense of life. The advantage that spiritual direction has over the journal is that there's somebody else there who can both tease out the greater meaning and challenge you on things. They can pull it out further than I'd necessarily do on my own. It's good to share my story with someone else; nice to know there's someone there who will sit and listen to me rabbit on. It's very affirming that my life and me are worth paying attention to. It helps me to pay attention to myself. It's a sorting and encouraging experience.'

The support that can be expected in both happy and sad events in ordinary life is described in this comment: 'Spiritual direction has helped me with family events and now with widowhood. I've realized how immature I am in many ways, but my director has congratulated me on overcoming it and that's helped. No one else does that.'

Freedom and release

For many people the gift of spiritual direction is simply the opportunity to off-load the weights that get in the way of living life in the full and free way they hope for. For example, 'It's having someone focused on me for an hour. That sounds very indulgent, but it is important. When you talk with friends you get ten minutes, then you have to listen to your friend in turn. Here you get an uninterrupted time to go through the layers. I find I get very deep, because I trust my director. I don't want to mess about. If I'm not going to be honest, I'm cheating myself. I don't sense any reticences, which is an incredible freedom. That doesn't happen with more than one or two people in my life.'

'It's been a focus time when I could talk about how it was for me. Most of the time you've got to keep that locked up and get on with what you're there to do. I am freer to be myself, whoever that is, with my director than with any other person in the world. This is a huge privilege. One of the griefs about losing my old counsellor is that he knew me in a way no one else does. With my present director I feel able to say anything and know that I am safe, that I needn't hold back (within the bounds of courtesy) because nothing has the power to hurt her as I could hurt someone in my family, no matter how dearly loved.'

'My director is the only person I've got for this sort of thing. I find it's calming. I feel sorted. It's like a safety valve on a pressure cooker. Everything is cooking hard. You put cold water on. All the fizz goes out and there is the lovely soup!'

Accompanying

The image of journey or pilgrimage is often used when people talk about their experience of direction. 'It is about having a guide who is herself on the journey, who is not going to think that anyone else's journey will be the same. The journey element itself is a powerful metaphor. Your director is someone who is walking with you; I like to feel an element of exploration. I need some kind of warmth, too.'

With the aspect of pilgrimage come echoes of Bunyan, as in this observation. 'My spiritual director has absolutely been a sheet anchor, solid, firm and there, someone who can be held on to. I have a certainty that the relationship won't be broken. It's the pathway (in the *Pilgrim's Progress*) along with my belonging to Church.'

It is, I hope, becoming clear that both parties in the direction relationship have their proper responsibilities. So I find it interesting to ask questions in a bit more detail about how people regard 'ownership'. What sort of influence – control even – should or can a director have over someone's life? A lay woman who herself accompanies others as a director described her own experience. 'Some directors think you should be very obedient. With a previous director I didn't find that helpful, because it went with an agenda. It took me time to realize what was happening and why I didn't feel comfortable. Obedience is to God and not to your director. I don't see my present role when I am directing others as requiring obedience to myself.' Her observation finds a response in these comments on the obligations on each party.

'The responsibility lies with the individual person. The key to direction lies in terms of helping. I find that reflection between the meetings is important. I bring things, not thinking, "My director will fix that", but, "She might have an angle on that." Her experience is there to draw on, to help me see things in a new light, from a different perspective. Nor am I conscious of my own present director telling me what I ought to be doing. I simply don't use words like that. It's never felt intrusive – a challenge sometimes, which is OK. Her questioning doesn't feel intrusive, because I want to go there. It would be more frustrating not to. I've been able to share as much as I feel comfortable with – at far greater depth than with anyone else except my wife.'

'God owns it. In the sessions God is there in control. I want him to be more in control before and after. I go along with my director's words because they resonate with what I have been feeling; it's not because I think her words are law.'

'It is important to try to understand where people are coming from and to be aware of their expectations. Sometimes these are not healthy; for instance when someone wants direct mentoring. A director needs to be deeply accepting and respectful of them; to allow them to grow in God's way and not necessarily the director's own way. I've not felt any intrusion. Spiritual direction is about two real people working together.'

Response

It is clear that listening is at the heart of the relationship in spiritual direction and that the experience of being properly heard has its own effect in healing hurts, in recognizing value or in clearing muddle. But there is also work for the director in responding to what he or she is hearing. Offering insights, reflecting back what has been said and occasionally giving advice are proper tools for a director to use in accompanying another person's journey. As a widow said to me, 'There is no one who will put me right now that I have no husband. He was often horrible to me, but he was also smart and wise, and he "corrected" me often when I needed it. My director hasn't done so yet, but I hope that if he saw me being wrong-headed, foolish or sinful he would have enough care and the right kind of love for me to say so. I have to trust in his disinterested charity. We can laugh and I can tease him. I do enjoy that. He's not the least pompous.'

Advice or counsel can come with different degrees of pressure for acceptance. Most often in spiritual direction the advice comes more in the form of suggestions inviting consideration than in the form of orders demanding obedience. There is a delicacy here, which was clearly put in this comment: 'There is an element of accountability and continuity, with being able to come and report back on what we talked about last time. Spiritual direction gives me a regular opportunity to reflect, to learn and to resolve things. Sometimes I go away thinking that it felt quite light. Other times there have been some big issues we've kicked around, which I needed to address. What helps is that spiritual direction can be objective and reflect back on things in a way that helps me see more balance. It is not a strongly prescriptive form of direction. It is more like an accompanying in reflection and co-operation with the Spirit. From time to time I take away a lot of wise words. Occasionally there are useful pictures of visual images. I've also found suggestions about books useful.'

The advice may come from the director's own experience or from his or her knowledge of the background to the spiritual life. This quotation from someone clearly on a spiritual journey is far from unusual. 'I'd had a spiritual high for a time and my director warned me that it wouldn't last. So, when later I was in the total spiritual dump, I felt, "Well, this is OK", because she'd warned me it was going to happen and told me I would come out of it at some point. "Helpful" and "good" are not quite the right words; it's about being reassured that you're going along a reasonable path. I can talk about things I wouldn't talk to many people about – if to anybody else. She always seems to unravel it, without ever minimizing the concern. I appreciate the prayer too, and the blessing and the hug. You need someone who is further along the journey than you are with a deeper spirituality to help you see what you're doing and where you're going.'

But it would be wrong to expect that coming to a spiritual director is coming to get advice that will sort out all life's problems. 'Spiritual direction is not about my coming to a trusted, older Christian, someone who's been a priest for many years, to get a blueprint for my life. It just ain't like that and that sort of thing is not going to work out anyway.'

In any case, one of the principles underlying the relationship in direction is that each person has a full responsibility for his or her own choices in life. A person may wish to share concerns and fly possibilities with the director, but it is finally up to that person to choose and to live out his or her choices. The following two quotations underline that principle:

'I've never felt he was saying, "You must do that and by the time you come back I shall want to hear that you have done so." He's much more an encourager than prescriber. I don't feel I'm answerable to him; I don't feel owned in my spiritual walk; I feel accompanied.'

'Responsibility always lies with the individual person. The key to the relationship is in terms of helping. I bring things, not thinking that my director will fix them, but that she might have an angle on them. My director's experience is there to draw on; she may see things in a new light, from a different perspective.'

Reassurance

If there was one word that came up more often than any other in the interviews I did in preparation for this book it was the word 'reassurance'. A feeling of inadequacy seems to be widespread among church people. It goes with a sort of belief or fear that 'out there somewhere' is the right way to be a Christian, a kind of blueprint that sets standards that the individual person simply cannot attain. I am not talking here about a deeply held, biblical understanding that we all fall short of the glory of God or that we are all only on the way to attaining the fullness of humanity that we see in the person of Jesus Christ. Rather, I refer to an attitude that I believe comes in the same family as a low self-esteem, a feeling of worthlessness or a background fear of rejection. My conversations with people suggest that one of the ways to meet the needs that these feelings indicate is to be found in the acceptance that a director offers in listening to someone's story.

A bank employee who has a lay ministry in her home church put it like this. 'I think of spiritual direction as being restorative; it builds you up and gives you strength. It's reflective; when you say out loud things about God and prayer and spiritual life, you find it gives you answers. It's refreshing; I always go away refreshed by drinking from someone else's spiritual cup, which is difficult in ordinary life. Sometimes it's quite challenging and I have to do some rethinking. I have experienced an unprecedented inner growth, which was prompted by life circumstances and relationships. I've found new thinking and awareness. Going to see a spiritual director has given me a real chance to look at deep issues and talk in an open-ended way about these things. There is a sense of support and safety; it's out of my home situation. There is no accountability to anyone except God and each other.'

Those comments are echoed by the mother of a family of small children. 'I suppose the term I'd use is "refreshment". I generally go home with something to cling on to, even if only a word. Holiness doesn't have to be a drudgery; it can be a joy. I've been through tantrums and joys and I've come to value life as it is. The sharing is lovely; English people don't normally go round talking about their inner thoughts. I find it very supportive, a good safety valve. Especially when I'm very low and things are desperate, it is good to share. It's very valuable: there have been occasions when being able to talk has saved a crisis and a real upset.'

The effect of the director's accompaniment is underlined in this comment: 'What it has given me is a sense of recognition, helping me to recognize where I am and why I feel as I do. It's given me encouragement that this is all quite normal and a reassurance that in some sense I am worthy – that there is work for me to do. I have often doubted that. My director helps me think through how I have got to where I am now and to evaluate how God has worked with me, through me, alongside me, even pushed against me sometimes. I couldn't have thought that through on my own; I needed the reassurance; since early childhood I haven't found much affirmation in many relationships. There's a basic insecurity in me that needs reassurance. Her encouragement has kept me going onwards and upwards; it's also given me confidence to question more. At times I feel very much a child in the faith and need guidance, assurance and reassurance.'

What helps

When I asked the people I interviewed what it was in the direction relationship that they found helpful, I received such a varied and interesting set of responses that I simply record them here without any attributions.

'It helps that I am the one who is accountable. I've heard spiritual direction described as "a compassionate mirror". Self-deception is a great danger in the spiritual life. God's compassion needs incarnating.

'There is no one else that I can talk to about these things except my director. They are too personal. Most of my friends and family are not Christians, and with the exception of one of them with whom I have touched a bit on these things, he is the only person who I can trust because he is wise, experienced and kind. It is also important to me that he still works at it, as it were. I'm sure he's not always right.'

'I like the midwifery image. My director has been through quite a few births with me. Gentle assisting with the birth, maybe not as messy as midwives sometimes get! I first came when I was at a crisis point and just needed to unload. I felt myself really welcomed in.'

'It's good when the director I have now gives a summary of where we've been at the end of a session; it's easier to go over it afterwards. My previous director's sessions were rather meandering. I prefer to be more businesslike.'

'It's important not to try to cover too much at once. The work is facilitated by being accepted as I am. Not many people in my life know me that well. No one sits down with me regularly like this, year in year out, to hear it all. There's something very liberating about that, just being able to be me and knowing that my director knows what I'm about. I feel I can say anything and be very honest – I am enabled to be honest. There's no point in pretending to be the person I'm not. Working together for so long makes that easy, because my director knows me and there's lots I don't have to explain. Not to mention all that good spiritual directors do in listening and reflecting back what you are hearing and what you think is going on.'

'I don't know how important it is, but it is helpful that my director and I are of an age, we have read and enjoyed a lot of the same books, we read the same papers; all that is a comfort and saves a lot of time and diagram drawing. I remember the first time my mother tried to kill herself; they made her see a psychiatrist who was so ill-educated that even references she made to things in common parlance and quotations from the classics were met by bewilderment and necessitated tedious explanations.'

'When I found a director, she was very patient with me, gently helping me to notice what was growthful and what was hindering, all the while emphasizing that what matters is availability to God. At various times over the years she has recommended helpful books, relating to the particular part of my journey, but her own presence, unconditional acceptance of me, and loving companionship on the way have been what have really helped. There have been times of deep struggle, conflicted questioning of my path and sometimes seemingly heretical tendencies. At these times of crisis I would come away from our meetings with my own sense of the rightness of my path affirmed, even though objective observation might yield a more questionable conclusion.'

'What I appreciate is being able to talk about God seriously and lay my life open to find out where God is leading me. I try to offer the best I can. It's really important to me to be doing what God wants. So I feel that grace is part of it, to sit and look at what is going on and build on what's good and avoid the traps I usually fall into – or at least get rescued from them.'

'I get a different perspective on it all, so I'm not just going round in circles on my own. Something new comes into the situation – another voice and different ideas. When I talk about work, it's refreshing to have a view from outside that world, another angle and a new eye on it.'

Counselling and spiritual direction

Of all the many and varied ways in which people are offered help in sorting out their lives, I suppose counselling is the most used. There is a range of resources that are based on psychological research and skill. Some, such as psychoanalysis and psychotherapy are intensive, with frequent sessions over a period of months or years. The various sorts of counselling tend to be less demanding than this, with fewer meetings over a shorter period. All the people who offer help in this way can be expected to have completed a serious course of training and to have reached a standard recognized by the professional body that regulates their particular discipline.

Counselling is different from spiritual direction in several ways. People seek counselling when they recognize that they have some severe difficulties or particular problems that they need to deal with. It usually involves sessions at least once a week and lasts for a limited time span. Spiritual direction offers a much more generalized accompaniment on the journey of life; it entails fewer meetings and is often open-ended. Counselling, except when it is specifically labelled as 'Christian counselling', has no specific Christian content.

Some spiritual directors are also qualified as counsellors and may work with people in both areas. However it is not unusual for people who are working with a director to come up against problems that are more appropriately worked with in the context of counselling than direction. Examples of the more serious problems that come beyond the scope of the spiritual director, although a director may be helpful and supportive, are serious addictions and the results of childhood abuse.

Among the responses of people I talked with are some from those who have experience of both sorts of help – counselling and spiritual direction.

'Spiritual direction is a different relationship from counselling. In counselling the aim is to help you to come to a resolution of what you're struggling with. Direction deals with your ongoing journey, which may at times encounter problems, but it is not problem-focused, which is a very different thing. Counselling and spiritual direction use the same or similar skills, but their focus and what you're about are totally different.'

'I have American friends who go to their shrinks frequently. It seems similar to what we do but without the spiritual dimension. I've tried to work out what the spiritual dimension is, but I find it hard to put into words. The spiritual dimension is about going deeper into my life, rather than running along on the surface. It has God at the root and heart of it all. I get the impression that counselling is more of a prop to get you through life, while spiritual direction is more like refuelling.'

'Counselling is very different; it goes on for a shorter

period to work on some particular area, while spiritual direction is to do with a relationship with a director as you grow and explore. It's is an ongoing thing. In counselling, faith doesn't necessarily come into it. Direction is concerned with your faith journey, in which prayer is a major part. But it is also about the practicalities of life. I've found that counselling takes no account of the Godward side. In spiritual direction we talk about prayer, God and ministry. It is part of my life in a way counselling was not. I got to know very little about the counsellor I went to, her journey, her life experience. My director and I have shared experiences; we have both experienced parish ministry. The biggest difference comes in the relationship – counselling is short-term as opposed to long-term direction. I feel my director is a companion on my Christian journey. I feel we connect, sometimes more than others. I value the listening, praying part. I have a sense of drawing away into a sacred space; the lighted candle says that for this hour we are together and the time is there to use, sealed with prayer at the end.'

'I had one or two sessions with a counsellor when my children were small. I don't really know where the line lies between the two. We use strategies and models in spiritual direction which counselling also uses. Our sessions have sometimes been spiritual direction and sometimes counselling. I can't see anything wrong with that; it depends on my needs at the time.'

'Counselling is more of a service or a treatment. If you feel something is wrong you go to a counsellor to sort it out. It's got that sort of focus to it. Spiritual direction, though I might come with a particular issue, is about the relationship with God. In spiritual direction you can share more of yourself. The counsellor is much more impersonal. In direction there is more conversation and dialogue.'

'I went for counselling because I couldn't cope with all that was going in the family. An example of the difference between counselling and direction is the way my first counsellor did not share my religious background and was out of her depth with my stuff. So I went to someone else who was more in tune. With my second counsellor I found that because of the professional relationship I didn't feel so free to be myself. We looked at the underlying psychological mix and things that were standing in my way. It was helpful, but I didn't feel that, although friendly and caring at the time, my counsellor really cared about me once the hour was up. All my directors up till now have been parish priests, deliberately so. I wanted it as part of normal churchgoing. Spiritual direction is more elastic and more of a relationship; it relies on both people and is honest and open. Counselling is more professional.'

The relationship

When I came to think about the kind of relationship that you find in spiritual direction, I kept coming back to the idea of friendship. There were other words such as 'ministry', 'companionship', 'profession' even, but even if it is a strange sort of friendship, that is the word I came to in the end. What makes for the strangeness is the imbalance. Usually friendship is something mutual, but that is rare in direction, as someone pointed out: 'My director is my friend but I am not his. He knows an awful lot about me and I know very little about him.'

A friendship

It is not always put as sharply as it was by the person just quoted; witness the churchwarden in a suburban parish who commented, 'It's the sort of friendship that gives a model for your relationship with God. I find I struggle over the same ground, probably not saying much different from what I said a couple of years ago. God isn't fed up with that and neither is my director. There is that sort of unconditional thing about it. It opens up a relationship of trust and love, which is supporting and helpful. It makes you think that God is like that. There is some mutuality, but the focus is more about me. It is a funny friendship. I do feel we are mutual friends and the mutuality is important for me, rather than any sort of professionalism. Spiritual direction is different from a professional relationship where a contract is needed. We do this work within our friendship, though it is useful to have someone outside the normal run of contacts as your director. It's good to get away from the ordinary and stand back to see what's happening from a distance. I'm more at home with the name "Spiritual director" than I am with "Soul friend". There clearly is a sense of friendship. I like, admire and trust my director and can't imagine direction without that. That immediately moves it outside of a commercial transaction. There is an important sense of trust and gratitude in the relationship. But I have come across older people whose experience of spiritual direction was colder, without much sense of friendship.'

A teacher in a secondary school described how she saw her director. 'I haven't got another relationship like it. I always believe my director prays for me and if you pray for someone you begin to love them, so she must love me. I dread the thought of her not being there – a bit like God! I've had all sorts of moves and changes in my life and I have been very lucky to have her there as a steady part of life; it has been a great help. I would say things to her that I wouldn't say to my best friend – I can imagine that happening. But then I wouldn't look to my director for relationships and activities that I would with my best friend.'

Sacramental aspect

As I wrote in the opening chapter, my own directors through my life have all been priests, and I have always regarded the work that I have done as a director as an integral part of my ministry as a priest. It has included confession and absolution when that has been asked for. However, I am convinced that in the ministry of spiritual direction, whether or not the director is ordained, God clearly uses the relationship and the conversation between two people as a means of grace. There can be no doubt of this when you hear the stories that they tell, like these two.

'It's important to me that my director is a priest, or at least acts in a priestly way. He comes over to me as someone who is deeply conscious that he is ministering grace. He doesn't have it in himself to solve my problems, so he won't try. But he will minister and that is important. Straightforwardly most of the time it is a delight to be in his company and when it isn't a delight it's because he is helping me to face things which, in another context, I have ways of avoiding. So there is that element of direction; the fact that he does direct is a necessary condition of the relationship.'

'It's not an ordinary friendship. My spiritual director is friendly, open and human and shares stories. She's not someone I see at other times; so there is a specialness about it. It's a spiritual friendship in a liminal place, like being on a beach; it isn't one thing or the other. You put yourself in a liminal place so that things can happen which might not happen in a more fixed place or more fixed relationship. There is space for the Holy Spirit; a space which is there when we meet and doesn't exist anywhere else. It's a friendship dedicated to God; that's what makes it spiritual and something different.'

Boundaries

There are limits in this special friendship. The boundaries are both practical and in the emotional, interpersonal sphere. They need to be recognized by both parties in the relationship.

A young man working as a designer said, 'I think boundaries are important. Your director is someone outside your ordinary life. This gives space in a way a friend doesn't. I need to know that my director is human; so it's OK to know a bit of her story, where she is coming from. But it is also important to know that the special space in spiritual direction won't be intruded upon by "friendship". Directors can sometimes introduce their own story helpfully; you realize you are not alone because others have similar experiences – so you're OK; you're not going dually. It helps to know the director really understands. But it's not like a normal friendship – it's a unique relationship.'

'I recognize there are boundaries. For instance I wouldn't ring at all hours or suddenly turn up on my director's doorstep. I think that maybe it's right that we don't meet socially. The relationship is a special one. I may learn a little about his life, but he's not using the session for his own spiritual direction.'

'Spiritual direction is a special relationship. The director is at the point of balance, looking openly at what's going on in me and my relationship with God, without her own agenda. It doesn't matter where that person comes from as long as she is able to be free, listening and objective. Boundaries matter and, of course, complete confidentiality makes it work. I value and trust in the director's confidentiality. I am actually an open person. I like to be able to share as much as I feel the need to. I couldn't do that with someone who I feared might use that information elsewhere. It's important not to mix roles, because if there is confusion, it can be painful and destructive.'

Using one's own clergy as directors

One of the boundary questions is whether a vicar should direct people from his or her own parish. With exceptions, the answer seems to be, generally, no. Most people prefer to have a director whom they are not going to meet regularly in other circumstances. Many clergy recognize the difficulties. Apart from the problems that can arise in individual relationships, many pastors find that they have difficulty in balancing the demands that their ministry makes on their time. Direction is time-consuming and other work may have priority. It also has to be recognized that it benefits from a certain amount of training and continuing support, which may not be available to all parish clergy.

An inner-city priest described his own practice. 'When parishioners want to go further in their faith life and come to me for help, I begin to meet with them for a while, but then I help them to find a spiritual director outside the parish. Otherwise there could be problems in the church community; there is so much confidential material and I am aware of the dangers of "the vicar's special friends".'

Guidelines

Then there are the limitations and boundaries that are properly observed in any pastoral relationship. Spiritual Directors International, which is based in the USA and has a largely US membership, has produced guidelines that deal with this subject under the heading of 'Dignity', emphasizing the the director's responsibility in:

- respecting the directee's values, conscience, spirituality, and theology;
- inquiring into the motives, experiences or relationships of the directee only as necessary;
- recognizing the imbalance of power in the spiritual direction relationship and taking care not to exploit it;
- establishing and maintaining appropriate physical and psychological boundaries with the directee; and
- refraining from sexualized behaviour, including, but not limited to, manipulative, abusive or coercive words or actions toward a directee.

These guidelines also underline that spiritual directors should maintain the confidentiality and the privacy of the directee by:

- protecting the identity of the directee;
- keeping confidential all oral and written matters arising in the spiritual direction sessions;
- conducting direction sessions in appropriate settings; and
- addressing legal regulations requiring disclosure to proper authorities, including, but not limited to, child abuse, elder abuse and physical harm to self and others.

Payment

The question of paying for spiritual direction comes up regularly and needs to be faced openly. There is a wide variety of expectation and practice. Some directors regard the work as a normal part of their ministry and do not expect to receive any money at all. At the other extreme the director may have given up other work to be available and needs proper remuneration. This is often the case with members of religious communities or with those who are engaged full-time in direction. Between these come the people for whom it is right to reimburse the expenses they incur. It may be embarrassing, witness these sentiments, shared by many other people: 'I wish the British could be more up-front about payment. I send a gift every time, but I'm never quite sure about it. Temperamentally I want on the one hand to be told something about how much, but on the other I don't like the idea of scales of fees and conditions of contract, which would change the relationship. I feel all along that my director has given herself and more than herself and in no sense have I been coming to buy her time. That would have given such a different character to what I needed in spiritual direction; I might as well have spent my money going to a management consultant.'

One man was very uncertain. 'Spiritual direction is quite trendy at the moment, which makes me suspicious. I don't like the idea of it being a commodity, something you can buy. It's a friendship and a relationship. You don't find most of your friends by applying to an agency. Thinking of spiritual direction as a commodity doesn't mean people shouldn't go for it.'

In contrast, another said: 'People should be paid for the time they give up. Money helps to show the value of the work. I feel quite comfortable about it. I think a contribution for expenses is fine, but strangely I find it difficult to tell other people about that. I suppose the financial question could be a sort of barrier.'

Again, 'It would be difficult to have to pay. There would be the element of professionalism; it would be best not to have to pay at the time of direction; to have a standing order with your bank, rather than sit and write out a cheque to give your director. But you can't ignore the fact that people have to live.'

Contracts

It is important that each party knows where he or she stands in this relationship. In some quarters you will find that some sort of contract or covenant is recommended.

Spiritual Directors International offers guidelines here. As in so many of the suggestions they make for conduct in direction, there are signs of a background in a society that is driven by litigation. In the UK such areas are often taken for granted. But there may well be some merit in talking them through with your director. Spiritual Directors International suggests that spiritual directors initiate conversation and establish agreements with directees about:

- the nature of spiritual direction;
- the roles of the director and the directee;
- the length and frequency of direction sessions;
- the compensation, if any, to be given to the director or institution; and
- the process for evaluating and terminating the relationship.

These themes were echoed in my conversations with people. 'My director agrees to meet me and listen to me at reasonable intervals. We have a review every now and then to check on how it's going.'

'There is an unspoken agreement. I trust my director's confidentiality so I feel safe. When I am working as a director myself, I find the length of times and the frequency of our meeting varies. It's usually an hour, but some people take much longer to unpack, up to two and a half hours. Some people find it hard to express their experiences, especially contemplatives.'

'Spiritual direction can't have the same contract system

as counselling, which is more intense. I think the language of contract is spurred by fear of litigation. But I suspect my director and I do have one, even if it is fairly unspoken. I recognize these points: I have a need, which she offers to meet. My director offers herself for me and God to address that need. It is clear we both understand what is happening. I retain responsibility for my own growth. I look for a compassionate mirror and some challenge. The way my director does that is not by being very directive, but sometimes she does offer a spur or provoke with a bit of "direction". There are two levels of directiveness: it can mean being interventionist during the session with comments, questions, etc, or it can mean interfering with what a person ought to do. The time limit of an hour is good; I feel I've done some work! The frequency is good too at about once every two months.'

This finds an echo from another person who told me she thought of any contract as being informal, 'but you need to make sure that the understanding matches what you are looking for. It includes things like identifying your needs for having direction, the frequency of meetings, confidentiality and any no-go areas, and an evaluative process from time to time.'

'We have a contract with several clauses. There is total confidentiality; no one knows apart from us. There is mutual respect; I know my director has nothing to gain or lose by telling me what I don't want to hear; if he doesn't tell me, it's because he has a good reason not to do so. He's not going to hold back for any irrelevant reason. There is a contract of faith.'

'I don't feel the need for a contract, as long as my director is aware of the need to review how it's working from time to time. We certainly don't have a written one. To begin with our sessions have been close together because of problems I was having to face. They will become further apart. Maybe the time will come when my present director is no longer helpful. I would accept a change if it was needed, but I don't like the idea of a time limit; as with God, it's one step at a time.'

'I find it works all right with an informal understanding that you know you can leave if the time is right to move on. Natural breaks happen. It is important that we have a review occasionally. I don't reckon we need a formal contract. I find that three months is a natural gap. Every now and then it's good to have a review session and ask, "Do you want to carry on?"'

'I like fixing the next date before I go. I know I could phone in an emergency and my director has the freedom to say he can or can't see me. On my side I will honour arrangements. It is important to establish a pattern. The risk is more on the director's side than on mine. It is a risky relationship. One of my directors I felt wanted me to go in a direction I violently disagreed with. So I left him, because it just didn't feel right. It is important to trust the Holy Spirit as the real director. You may have to take a stand like that and say, "No, this is not the right way. However much I respect you as a spiritual director, I must find someone else." It took me some time to get there, as I'm not very confident.'

'I think we have an agreement. I feel quite a strong

sense of obligation to be as honest as I can. I think I have more the sense that this is a ministry that my director offers me; and in the very offering there is an invitation rather than an obligation for me to take it up. It has the element of grace about it. I don't want to make a contract to meet a certain number of times a year, but I am glad we've made a date for next time before we part.'

'I don't think I want a contract. I suspect the idea comes from the American zeal for litigation. It's not that kind of relationship – or at least I don't experience it like that. If we got to the point where I wasn't receiving anything in this ministry, then I would say so. It would be ridiculous to blame anyone.'

A friend who works as a spiritual director has been seeing two or three people for a good long time. He wonders whether they would benefit from a change. 'Sometimes you have to move on. You change and need a different sort of help.'

Snags

As in any relationship things do not always go smoothly. People noted some of the difficulties and dangers which need to be guarded against.

'I am aware there could be a danger of becoming too comfortable and just having cosy chats, but I haven't found it so. There's still that edge. I am aware of the presence of God in it and that stops the cosiness. I find that the intensity of our meetings varies with the various situations in my life.'

'Over-dependence could be a difficulty. There have been times when I don't know how I'd have got through without spiritual direction. At the other extreme there could be a failure of trust with an emotional hold over people, or a hold over them by knowing so many things about them.'

'I wouldn't want someone who sets their own agenda, someone who doesn't really listen to what I am saying, someone who is manipulative. Equally I wouldn't want a director who has it all buttoned up and has all the answers. I'd be wary of a very intense relationship, and I wouldn't want someone who knows very intimate things about me, someone I'm likely to meet all the time.'

'I don't find sharing a drawback; sometime it's painful, but I know I need to. I want to be totally open and honest with God; that's better than living a lie to myself. I believe everyone should have a spiritual director. God wants barriers broken down, leading to a relationship of real intimacy. However painful it might be, a session shows whether you mean business or not.'

'My discomfort comes from facing up to things. I bring stuff which I am unsure, unhappy or bothered about; things which cause a blockage in relation with God. I bring my pain. There is a danger of not being as honest as one should, which destroys the purpose of it.'

'Our regular meetings make me think – not that I have to give an account to my director, but they remind me what is happening, what I am becoming, how I am doing. It is not so much that the director says, "You ought to", more, "Why don't you?"'

'What I find hard is when I am dealing with something quite difficult, where I am wrong and need to deal with it. I look for that combination of integrity and sensitivity in my director – a difficult blend. And then there's the worry about, "Does any of this that I am talking about make sense?"'

One of the areas that raises questions is whether a director may be over-directive. 'I have looked to my director for direction. I remember the early meetings, when it would not have helped if she had been non-directive. I would have felt that this person was not taking me seriously enough. So I appreciated it when she said things like, "What seems to me to be going on in your life is so and so, and what I think you ought to begin to think about is so and so." Because she did just that there was a sense of direction, but not direction as instructions, which would have turned me off.'

The director as teacher

In the relationship there is for many people a strong element of learning and growing, which gives the director something of a teaching role. However there are many different ways of describing the nuances of this side of the ministry.

'I regard my director more as an accompanier and elucidator than primarily as a teacher. In our sessions it's not like direct teaching but more nudges and winks, and I find that her suggestions and questions have eased me on without it ever appearing to be overt teaching.'

'It is significant that my director has taught me things that I would now judge to be absolutely crucial, except that I knew them before he taught them to me! An earlier director said, "Find space; don't exhaust yourself"; and so on. Now it's more like Dr Johnson's aphorism, "It is not sufficiently considered that men need more to be reminded than to be informed".'

'Education happens. My director's interventions show an understanding of the issues, which is educative and reinforces what I am learning, adding something useful. Stories from his own or other people's experience, told appropriately, have a lesson in them.'

'Yes, education is part of it. But I find midwifery is a helpful image. The midwife encourages and enables the process of birth. The labour is the woman's; it is she who brings the child to birth. The midwife accompanies, helps and guides; she gives education and advice if need be.'

'Over the five years my director has been a guide to me and manifestly along paths he knew. Elements of teaching have been important, but it has always been relevant, sensitive and by way of invitation. He saw more clearly what was happening to me when I described my life, without being in any way judgemental or dismissive – nor letting me be too hard on myself as I became judgemental and dismissive.'

Summary

This chapter and the previous ones are an attempt to survey a very wide field. Just as no two personalities are the same, so no two relationships in spiritual direction will have the same features. The quotations have been drawn from different people's experience and so present, with the commentaries, a rather richer mixture than one individual is likely to meet. However, I trust that there is enough evidence of what may be possible in spiritual direction for readers to decide whether to go ahead and find their own guide. Help for that enterprise is offered in the next chapter.

Finding and choosing a director

Once you have decided that it would be right for you to find yourself a spiritual director, there are a number of different ways of going about it. One important piece of advice, though: take your time to be as sure as you can that the relationship is going to be helpful. There is rarely any hurry to choose someone who will be the right person for you. It is an important decision for you to make and there is no need to rush. It may not be easy to find someone. As someone who had a number of different directors because of moving round the country said, 'A real difficulty can be finding the right person. I find it takes about a year to settle down before you can be sure that you have. You recognize by a certain intuition that that's the one to go for.'

Many people are put in touch with the man or woman who eventually becomes their director through personal contact. In the British spiritual direction scene there is no overall organization responsible for lists of accredited or authorized directors. Indeed, you will often find that those who are involved in the work recoil from such an idea. So you cannot go to a directory and look up names as you might for other help. There is no classification in the

Yellow Pages! But the first step many people take is the same as looking for a good plumber. If you ask around your friends you may well find one who recommends a firm that has done good work for her.

You could start by asking people in your church. Your priest or minister may well know someone to suggest or may be able to put you in touch with a suitable network. Spiritual direction in the UK is not highly organized. In many parts of the country there are training courses for people who want to become directors, most of them run on an ecumenical basis, and their leaders may be able to recommend people. In some parts of the country Church of England dioceses and other churches have advisers in spirituality, who may keep lists of directors and can make introductions. You may find there is a local group of directors who meet for fellowship and ongoing training, based on a retreat house or church training centre; so it is worth asking the Principal or the Warden there for help.

Although there is no national list of authorized or accredited spiritual directors, as you could find for professional counsellors, the Retreat Association co-ordinates a regular meeting of people concerned with the training of directors. They also facilitate a sort of exchange between people who are looking for a director and those in their locality who might be able to introduce them to one. The Retreat Association also produces a useful pamphlet on 'Choosing a Spiritual Guide', from which I have drawn several ideas for this chapter. (Their address is The Retreat Association, The Central Hall, 256 Bermondsey Street,

London SE1 3UJ; <www.retreats.org.uk>; tel: (020) 7357 7736; e-mail: info@retreats.org.uk.)

Choosing a director

By now you will have realized that the relationship between someone and his or her spiritual director is a delicate one. It is important to get it right. Pray about it, do some homework on it and trust your own instincts and reactions. And do not be in a hurry about it; take your time to get it right.

The earlier chapters may have helped you to sort out your reasons for wanting a director. It might help to write them down. You may also have an idea of the kind of person you are looking for, the kind of small ad you would write – 'WLTM SD with GSOH', perhaps.

Are you looking for a man or a woman, a priest or a lay person, a religious sister or a monk or friar? Do you want someone who belongs to the same denomination as yourself or who comes from the same tradition within your church? Or would you prefer to look for someone from a different stream? What about age, someone older or younger than yourself? Then there is the question of familiarity; would you prefer someone you already know or are likely to meet in other contexts, or someone who is new to you and not within your own circle at all? As you read that list of questions, notice your reactions. Which areas seemed to matter and which seemed irrelevant? If you stay with the important questions, you are beginning to build a profile of the kind of person you feel could help you, though it should not be too sharp or exclusive. God can often spring surprises.

You may not always have the same set of criteria. People and circumstances change. One woman said to me, 'At different times I have needed a different sort of director. I got so much from the first woman I went to. I explored all sorts of things with her which wouldn't come up with a man, but I have never met another woman I should like to be my director.'

A Free Church minister, speaking about her director told me, 'It is significant that we come from different traditions. I can't imagine another minister as my spiritual director. All the ministers from my own denomination I know who have had spiritual directors have had people outside the tradition, which indicates the importance of a view from outside the situation.'

Practical matters

Simple questions such as 'where?', 'when?' and 'how long?' need to be asked. The place where you meet for direction needs to be convenient; think how far you are prepared to travel. The frequency of meetings will depend, quite simply, on how often you need to meet. You will want to work this out with your director. I have found that some people like to meet less than twice a year, some like to meet every month, with most people somewhere in between, at four or five times a year at intervals of about two or three months.

The length of a session is usually about an hour. Sometimes it needs to be longer, but not so long that either party gets exhausted. Sometimes it can be shorter if there is less to talk about or one or other of you is very tired.

A second 'how long?' question is about the length of the relationship itself. Both the enquirer and the director realize that it will probably take several meetings before each knows whether or not it is going to work. So it is generally recognized that you begin with a period of probation. After a certain number of meetings, you review together what has happened during that time and decide whether it is right to continue or whether the time has come to look for another person as your director. If you do not feel that the person you are seeing is right for you, you need to say so – and to realize that this is perfectly proper and acceptable.

Place

Spiritual direction can happen in all sorts of places: your own home, your director's study or office, a church, a side chapel, a room in the church hall, a convent sitting room – all these sorts of locations have their own feeling, some more helpful than others. People vary in their opinions about the place, but most say that their own home is not a good venue. There are too many distractions to filter out, such as family, door bells and phones.

For some it is particularly helpful that the meeting takes place in a place with strong religious links, as in this instance: 'Meeting in a church is meeting in a place of prayer. I notice, like a call, the lighting of a candle, a moment of recollection. In the chapel there's a sense of drawing away from busyness outside. A lack of distraction is most important. I was glad that something like that was happening rather than just, "Sit yourself down and make yourself comfortable".'

Others prefer a room that is more homely. 'The place of meeting does make a difference. It needs to be a bit separate. I would rather be in a comfortable, intimate, familiar sort of room than sit very formally in a chapel with a prie-dieu. I appreciate somewhere that is homely, welcoming and relaxed. It's easier sitting comfortably and talking in a fairly quiet and peaceful place without distractions.'

The choice of venue can also carry deeper meanings. 'I am grateful that the early meetings were in my director's home, because I felt then – whether she meant it or not, I don't know – that she was giving me herself. This was important territory for her and she asked me to come and share it with her. I found that was very important and indicative of this confidence. This person is not just doing a job here; this is a way of life; something she is.'

There is certainly some advantage in having to travel to meet. 'Place doesn't make much difference to me because the relationship is firm. It is good to go to the director's place, as it opens space for me. His study feels friendly and homely and I enjoy the journey there. I need that further hour driving home to to go back over the meeting. It's like having a lawn in front of a house; I need the space to stand back and reflect and think through what's gone on. There's a lot of preparation too. So it's much more than just the hour we meet. One needs time afterwards for transition from the session to what you do next. The distance I have to travel to our meetings is costly in terms of time. But I can use the journey to think. In one's own house there is the danger of interruptions.'

Preparation

When you meet with a possible director for the first time, it helps to spend some time in preparation. So I suggest quiet reflection before a first meeting to think what it is that you are hoping to get from it. Think how you would like to tell your story, the things about yourself and your life that seem to you to be important, your hopes and joys, fears and pains. There may also be events and relationships from the past that stand out. Then put into words, if you can, who or what God is for you and what God means for you. Notice your own journey in faith with the high points and the low points, and whether you notice any changes going on in your spiritual life. See if you can put into words what it is that has brought you to ask for spiritual direction and how you would describe your needs and your hopes. Some people find it helpful to make some notes to take along with them.

Naturally the same is true for subsequent sessions. Most people find it helpful to prepare before a session and then to take some space afterwards to review what has been said and heard. These comments from a number of people show a range of different practices and may suggest some ideas.

'I have a book with me to note things I want to air and afterwards to note down what I have aired. I prepare beforehand most times. I try to put things in priority, and that helps to sort out my own life. So even before we meet, the process of spiritual direction has begun. It's on my mind a lot beforehand as I prepare for the meeting. But the last few times I have had such turmoil that it all pours out in the first ten minutes. Later it calms down.'

'I find that there are times when I am so rushed I don't have space to do any preparing before we meet. When we begin I wonder what on earth we are going to talk about and when I leave I realize we have dealt with some very important stuff in our conversation.'

'I think it's important not to try to look at too much at once. I prepare in an ongoing reflective way, pondering over quite a long period while I'm driving or in the bath. Then I digest by letting it just roll around. Usually things fall into place. I find it works better not to be too organized; I'm a naturally reflective person.'

Summary

The main chapters of this book should give you a good idea of the things to be sensitive about when it comes to deciding whether the person you are meeting is likely to be the right director for you. There is the absolutely basic area of trust. Do you sense that anything you say will be held in confidence? Does he give you the impression that he may be able to help you – that he knows what spiritual direction is all about? Then there is the question whether you feel comfortable with this person. Is she interested in you and your story? Do you feel welcome there? What sorts of body language do you notice? Are you being given full attention? I realize that something was not as it should be when I hear comments like, 'He didn't switch the phone off, so our time was continually interrupted by him answering calls', or 'I couldn't help noticing that she yawned a lot when I was talking.'

The business of finding a director may take quite a long time. Partly this may be because of the practicalities of knowing how to look for one, but there are all sorts of personal resistances that come into play; for instance, 'I capitulated to having a spiritual director kicking and screaming. As a "good evangelical", I resisted human help in my prayer life. What could a person teach me that was more than the Holy Spirit himself? However, in the end my frustration outweighed my resistant thinking. I had encountered a contemplative or two, been seriously impressed by the serenity, love and Christlikeness in their lives, and knew I wanted these qualities in mine. So, like a proper American and evangelical, I set out to achieve the prayer of silence with the help of a few books. A year later, no further forward and at the end of my tether with frustration, I gave in and asked a friend for help in finding a director.'

Then there is the area of faith and the difficult judgement about whether your possible director has her own deep faith and whether you can sense that she is committed to her own journey. To put it starkly, the question is whether you can see signs of holiness, however you yourself may define the holy. Intuition plays quite a large part in that sort of judgement.

If it matters to you, you may need to ask about the kind of training she has taken as a director, what her church background is or whether she follows any particular school of direction.

Praying

By now it will be clear that spiritual direction is concerned with the whole of life. It will also be clear that I believe that the whole of life is God's concern. Prayer is a special way of expressing the relationship between a person and God. So it is quite proper that a part, often a large part, of the work that goes on in a time of direction should be concerned with what happens when someone prays. In this chapter I offer a description of the many ways that different people find they are able to express that relationship.

I have included similar chapters in previous books I have written; so if you have read one of them, you may find some repetition. However, I think it is helpful to go over this ground again for two reasons. The first is that I have found it very useful as a director to use these ideas in an early meeting when a new person comes to me, to help them to recognize the value of their way of praying and the possible routes they could follow as it develops. The second is that I hope it will help readers who may not have reflected in this way before to do the same.

First, though, a really important piece of advice. Do not feel forced into praying in a way that does not seem natural for you. A well-worn maxim says, 'Pray as you can and not as you can't'. There are all sorts of models for prayer. Many people carry with them patterns from earlier stages in their journey of faith or ideas that they have picked up from books or from authoritative teachers. These patterns and models may work well. On the other hand, they may be inappropriate for them, but they may also be very hard to shake off without strong feelings of guilt, as a friend wrote to me: 'How do you guide people to what is right for them? We were taught to pray when we were young and, even if we can no longer do it that way, it has left a residue, a pattern which still haunts us. I am fascinated that this human race has this long history of dissatisfaction with prayer. After all, the disciples asked Jesus how they ought to pray even though as pious Jews they had certainly been taught how to do it. Nobody seems to be really satisfied with how he or she prays.'

A director will seek to help people to recognize the value of what happens here and now in their prayer and how they might grow in it. A great director of the early part of the twentieth century, Baron Friedrich von Hügel, used a French word, *attrait*, to mean that manner of praying that draws people and attracts them; the way that they find suits them and that at this time in their life is right for them.

Although I recognize that there are some for whom prayer is not focused in this way, I believe that most men and women who are set on growing spiritually and are committed to the journey need to develop a practice of regular praying. There is real value in setting aside a time for it. In the pages that follow, I am thinking specifically of the various ways in which the time could be used and how the different aspects of our personality are brought into play.

A number of ministers in a friend's church come to talk with him. The theme that runs through so much of what they have to say is, 'It's so busy, I'm so tired; so I don't pray – because that's one more thing to fit into the schedule.' My friend points out that at that stage they have missed it! If prayer is just one more segment of the pie chart, it's unreal from the start.

There are, of course, many other important occasions when we pray. Prayer is a corporate event as well as a private one. Church worship and the celebration of liturgy are very important parts of the Christian's journey. For many people it is useful to join with other people and pray together, either with just one other person or in a small group.

Prayer map

When I am working with people in this area, I have a sort of map to help sort out which of four *attraits* speak to someone (see Figure 1). One area is where prayer is largely expressed in words and where patterns and systems are important. One is where prayer is concerned with thinking and the use of 'the front part of your mind'. One is where prayer uses and is worked on by feelings and emotions, where the senses are important and where it can be expressed in practical, physical or artistic ways. And one is where prayer is no longer active, but receptive and where silence and availability are the keywords.

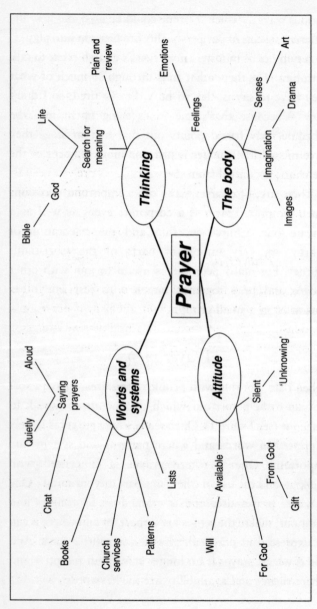

Figure 1. Prayer map

As you read through the fuller descriptions that follow, you may find it useful to notice both where you recognize something of your own experience and also where what you read is quite foreign to you. Remember, we're not talking about right and wrong here. The map is simply descriptive. It outlines what happens in practice, how people actually pray. There is no way in which it tells people how they ought to pray. You may also notice that there are parts of the map that describe where you used to be in the past – parts to which your journey once took you and has now led you away from.

Prayer as words and systems

'Saying prayers' is how most people describe praying. It is how most of us were first taught about it. If prayer is a relationship with God, then it is natural that we express it in conversation. So people talk to God, sometimes aloud, probably more often in their heads, about all sorts of things that are important to them. A good many people find that this kind of conversation takes place not only during specific prayer times but runs through the day as a kind of chat with 'a friend up there'.

Books of prayers are to be found in shops and at the back of churches. Some people find them a great help, either to read and use just as they are or to draw ideas from for making up their own prayers. Other people create their own book of prayers, which they collect from other sources or write for themselves.

In the prayer map, I link systems and patterns with the

attrait using words in prayer. Christians belong to the community of the Church and the way this is expressed is by joining in the worship that is offered by the community. Going to church, taking part in services, often with the Eucharist at the heart of it, may be the way in which a person's prayer comes alive. For these people there is a real satisfaction in being part of something bigger than themselves. In this common prayer they recognize that they are being carried by the community and at the same time expressing what it means to be an active member of that community.

It may also be important to have a firm pattern to the way you pray in private. One of the simple outlines for prayer is 'ACTS'. 'A' stands for adoration, voicing our wonder at God in his glory and his love. 'C' is for confession; faced with God's goodness, we need to express our sorrow for our sins and accept his forgiveness. 'T' for thanksgiving comes next as we recognize all the good things in our life. 'S' is for supplication as we ask God for the things that other people and we ourselves need.

Lists of people and causes to pray for may feature highly in this way of praying. The work of intercession is a recognized part of our relationship with God, and for some people this is helped by having things written down. You may pray with your own list of people who matter to you as a reminder. It may be a list for every day or a list that includes daily and weekly intentions. Churches often have printed lists of local needs or world-wide links. Missionary societies and other groups send out their lists. In fact, there are so many possibilities that you may well have to work out your own priorities and see which are most important for you, not unlike choosing between the hundreds of charities that send out Christmas appeals for support and catalogues of possible presents.

Prayer as thinking

For a large part of our waking day we are using our mind to work things out, to understand questions and to resolve difficulties. We spend a good deal of energy acquiring information and assessing data in order to make choices and decide what to do. Some people find that it is these skills that they mainly use in prayer. For them prayer is about working things out and making sense of the questions that faith and life present. There can be very few who have not tried to face up to the big challenges that being a Christian presents. We have to face the problems that come when we proclaim a belief in a loving God and at the same time are overwhelmed by the suffering and injustice in the world we live in. There are the big, global questions and there are the personal, private and family events that we need to figure out with God.

In this search for meaning the Bible has a special place. Many Christians give a good deal of their daily prayer time to reading, studying and pondering over a passage of Scripture. Often they follow a scheme of readings or a set of daily notes. For instance, in the Anglican Church, as in others, some people use the lectionary, which selects passages for reading at Morning Prayer and Evening Prayer. The basic work of this kind of prayer is to understand more deeply what the gospel has to say to you and to see what implications that awareness has on the way you live your life, shape your attitudes and make your choices and decisions.

I find that for many people, perhaps men especially, prayer is largely concerned with practicalities. It is about the choices for action that everyday life throws up and how to live out what it means to be a Christian in the relationships of work and neighbourhood, home and family. Prayer in the morning looks ahead to the day, with its events and meetings with people, and offers these things to God for his blessing and for his help in living out his will in them. This is balanced by prayer in the evening, taking some time to review the day that has passed, recognizing what has happened and how you have reacted; it is an opportunity for noting with thanksgiving the gifts and for making an act of repentance for your failures during the day.

Prayer and the body

We are physical beings. Our bodies play a very large part in our prayer. So do other aspects of ourselves, which I shall deal with here, though they are not exactly physical. Our five senses, our feelings and emotions, and our imaginations are all involved to a greater or lesser extent. It works both ways. Your body has an effect on how you pray, and you can express your praying through your body. The same goes for your emotions and for your different senses. As with the other *attraits* some people will feel more at home with this section than others.

So how does your body affect the way you pray? You have probably noticed that when you are not well it is harder to pray. Physical health or illness have their effect on spiritual life. The way you position your body also seems to have an effect too. Generations of children knew the teacher's call to prayer as, 'Hands together, eyes closed'. Standing, sitting, kneeling or lying down are all possible positions to pray in. Having your hands folded, open on your lap or held up in the air can express different attitudes to God. Again there is no right or wrong way; you have to find out for yourself what is most helpful.

One thing is worth pointing out. There is a recognized link between your back and your prayer. I am never sure what it means to describe prayer as 'easier' or 'harder', but most people understand the difference. It is a general experience that if you are sitting down to pray, it is easier if you are upright with both feet on the floor and your bottom tucked into the back of the chair. There is something about having your spine as vertical as it will go. Slouching deep in a comfy armchair is not a good way to start to pray.

You might like to ask yourself what word your position is saying – what it is that your body, your arms and legs and head, express in relation to God. Words that come to mind include 'alert', 'submissive', 'joyful', 'loving', 'penitent', 'available', 'receptive', 'keen'. You will be able to think of others.

As well as helping or hindering prayer, your body can also express itself through the position you are in, or through movements of your hands, or by bowing low to the ground, or through dance; anything, in fact, that you find meaningful.

Senses

We experience the world around us through our five senses, and our perceptions are continually having their effect on us. As they trigger all sorts of other actions, it is natural that they trigger prayer. Beautiful views, the sound of music, the feel of rosary beads in your fingers, instant memory smells – all of these can lead into prayer. Equally it is through using our senses artistically that we can respond prayerfully in all sorts of ways. It could be musically, in singing or playing on an instrument or in drawing, painting with colours or working in clay.

Emotions

Feelings and emotions are a large part of our life and it is natural that they are also integral to our praying. Gratitude or anxiety, fear or loving, as well as many other feelings, may be the starting point for prayer. Notice how big a part your feelings play in your own prayer. You may recognize both how often emotions generate prayer and how far you are able to express your feelings in your praying. You have only to read a few of the psalms to realize that this is not a recent phenomenon.

Drama

Imagination, fantasy and day-dreaming are also an important element in many lives. They can also have their place in prayer. In particular I am thinking about a way of praying with the Bible that St Ignatius of Loyola suggested. The idea is that you take a quite short passage of a Gospel to work with. Choose a story, something Jesus did or said, a miracle or a parable perhaps, and read it gently. As you read, relax and in your imagination find yourself there in the place of the story; sense the scene, the surroundings, the sights and sounds, the smells even. Notice the people who are concerned and what is going on. Again, in your imagination, take part in the action or the conversation and hear what Jesus may be saying to you yourself in it. Let this lead you more deeply into prayer, to a being with Christ, or to some realization of what you might do in response to this time of prayer.

Silence and attitude

So far I have described fairly active ways of praying. They are not without times of listening or being aware of what is beyond yourself, but in general in these methods it is the praying person who takes the initiative and talks or thinks or expresses feelings. Now I want to look at a way of prayer that is more passive, more receptive.

It is the prayer of silence, the prayer of an attitude of willingness to be available to God. It is known as contemplative prayer or contemplation. It is when you spend a period of prayer time centred on God in silence. It is when words seem not to be necessary; they may even get in the way. It is the same with thinking. Somehow you do not need to work things out in this way of prayer; it is more about relationship than about solving problems.

Feelings and sense perceptions may help in leading us into contemplative prayer, but in the prayer itself they are often more of a hindrance, obscuring the true purpose, which is a simple offering of your will to be there for God. A wise and holy nun described it as, 'Not so much trying to love God as letting God love you.'

It is in looking at contemplation that I am most aware that there are some readers who will at once recognize what I am writing about, while others may well find it quite foreign. This underlines what I said at the start. Different people pray in different ways and prefer to use or express different aspects and abilities of their personality. My hope is that you may have found some points in the descriptions that ring true for you. Recognize that this is probably where you are meant to be at present.

In conclusion

You may have realized that some of the notes describe a place where you used to be but have since moved away from. Just as in other aspects of human life there is change and development, so in prayer you can expect to move from one *attrait* to another as time goes on and you meet with different experiences. Many of the changes will take place easily and you may only realize they have happened when you look back.

The change towards contemplative prayer is one that very often causes problems and confusion for people. I believe it is a time when it is really very helpful indeed to work with a spiritual director who can accompany you along this new path of your journey. Indeed I think it is so important that I have devoted the next chapter to the kinds of openings and difficulties that you can find in this transition.

Growing into quiet

In earlier times, contemplative, mystical prayer was thought of as the preserve of monks and nuns in enclosed orders, something for people who were helped by the life of a monastery or convent and had the space to develop this aspect of spirituality. It is clear, both from twentieth-century writing and from the people we meet in today's Church, that there is a far wider field than that. Indeed the promotion and support of contemplative prayer is in some places a real growth industry, while in others we hear complaints that it seems to be a hidden secret: 'Our clergy never talk about it.' There are different words for the kind of prayer we are talking about. It could be contemplative prayer, the prayer of silence, apophatic prayer, *via negativa*, centring prayer or mystical prayer. And that list does not take account of all those franchising titles that get added to denote a particular school, tradition or teacher.

People may come to contemplation through imaginative prayer, the exercise of the emotions, or any of the other ways of praying. But contemplative prayer is very different from vocal prayer or meditation in that it is passive rather than active; rather than words or thoughts it uses silence. It is about an attitude of willed choice to be available to God and very little else. There is virtually nothing to do. The key points are God's gift, grace, and the person's being open to receive.

Discerning signs of transition

People come to a director for help, or at least for understanding, when they feel something has gone wrong with their prayer – it doesn't work as it used to, they can't concentrate on their meditation, the feelings they were accustomed to seem to be dead, and they hark back to the warmth in prayer they used to enjoy. They are frustrated, angry and upset. They express guilt at the lack of success in their spiritual life, because clearly they must be lazy; they are not trying hard enough. They fear that they are losing God or that they have to face the fact that they have lost God. (It may be, of course, that they have had to let go of an old, worn-out God.) There can be a further fear in all this too: 'Does God really love me or was it all a false hope?' There is distress that prayer is no longer what it used to be; it's boring; it feels like a waste of time. Something has been lost and it is very sad and confusing. Prayer has become empty and dry and all you can do is fidget. Why not just give it up? However, it is not always doom and gloom like that for everyone. There are people for whom the move into silent, passive prayer is accompanied by a sense of deep joy, of overwhelming love, or of the close presence of God.

'When I had my experience of the Holy Spirit, I didn't

react as so many others did. I wasn't into hand-waving stuff. For me it was an inner thing. I found that my director could tell me that what was happening in my prayer life as I moved into contemplative prayer was OK; it was normal. I hadn't gone weird. Spiritual direction was having someone to encourage me to go on in the way I felt I was being led and that it was all right, not odd or way off-beam. He helped me to put things into words and say, "This is what it's all about." I recognized that it wasn't just me and that there was a whole spiritual tradition here.'

A young woman in a mothers' and toddlers' group told me, 'I give myself a bad time over my prayers.' She wanted to pray, she wanted to be close to God, but she was trying too hard to get there. She felt it was all her own fault that nothing seemed to be happening. As the group spent a long time looking at what prayer meant to them, several of them came to realize from their own experience that for all their confusion and the demands of their small children, what they were being given in their prayer was the grace of silence and emptiness, something much more important than a lot of satisfying thoughts and feelings. What they taught me was to be on the alert for the signs of a person trying so hard that he or she is unable to recognize God's gift. People do not give themselves a bad time over prayer unless it matters to them. It shows that they really are committed to the search when they feel such pain at what appear to be blockages in their way.

The language that people use can provide a clue.

Talking about the times of prayer in which they are experiencing all this upset and confusion, they use double negatives. It's not that God is present (as perhaps God used to be experienced in the earlier days), but God is certainly not absent.

Contemplative prayer runs counter to so much of our contemporary Western culture. Around us, what matters is succeeding, getting to the top, making lots of money, achieving, and winning. There is a vast market in books telling you 'How to be a better...' Nor are these goals absent in the cultures of various churches. I think of the worship of second and third academic or professional degrees, not to mention the competition among professionals over size of church rolls and the scale of church finances. Here in contemplative prayer we have an attitude that says that neither self-fulfilment nor acquisition is the main aim of the human being. Rather it is the attitude of passive waiting and availability that leads to the loss of self in openness to the love of God and to its expression in practical love of one's neighbour.

Probing a little deeper, one may find that the challenging question, 'What is your deepest desire?' leads to important, revealing answers. Often people are a bit embarrassed to admit that they want to pray, not necessarily for the excitement or even the fulfilment, but because God matters so much to them. They want God. You may notice also that people talk about gradually getting used to the silence, finding in it a wordless security, a calm centredness. In all this they may be aware of a longing simply to be there for God.

'The time when my director said, "Just sit there and be quiet", and the phrase, "I am here for you", have meant so much. I have discovered the glorious ambiguity of who is saying those words, although she didn't say so. I'm here saying it to God and there comes a moment when it is God saying it to me, and the thing is transformed. Like Archbishop Ramsey being asked how long he prayed and answering, "Two minutes, but it takes me 25 minutes to get there." There's the stillness and the quietness and the relating, and I am for the moment in a world that is transformed and the glory of God really is a human being. All that exploration has behind it and within it a very sound theology without theologizing. There is a certain simplicity to it.'

To quote a nun friend: 'I am so aware that contemplative prayer only really begins when you turn a somersault and you find the only doer is God. Your role is simply to *be* consent to the action (like sunbathing). It is very easy to think the means is the end and I question whether directors keep the goal clear and stark enough. It is necessary to let go of "*I* surrender" or "*I* consent"; instead it is a matter of becoming consent.'

Surprisingly there is often a problem with silence itself. When the activity of thinking, planning, getting worried or upset and all the rest calms down and you are left with 'the prayer of loving regard', time passes in a different way. You may come to the end of 15 minutes of being still and wonder what has been happening. You don't seem to have been asleep, but were you? We are so used to doing things that about the only time we are not active is when we are asleep, so it is not surprising that when we move into deep inactivity and into receiving, it feels so close to sleep. Again the director's question may be, 'Where was God in that time? Present? Absent? Or perhaps, not absent?'

Another clue may come up after a while. People may find that if they do not keep their regular time of prayer over a number of days, they become aware that they really are missing it. The guilt they used to feel at not keeping up their rule subtly changes to sense that they have missed an opportunity to be there with God.

Then, among the signs to watch for in the work of contemplative prayer, there are the effects that may be seen in the rest of life outside the prayer time. People may notice that after a while their perceptions generally become sharper. They may feel more together as a person, less self-conscious. Patience may come more easily. Other people may even notice!

In a short collection of haiku poems from the Benedictine sisters at West Malling in Kent, there are these two poems, which point to the different experiences to be regularly found in contemplative prayer:

> Prayer? A waking heart,
> activity of stillness,
> live inter-presence.

> Prayer? Empty wasteland,
> dull heart, God nowhere found:
> mute perseverance.

Accompanying

Coming to the director's part in this journey, I find myself wanting to write 'Less is More' in very big letters. It really is a matter of discerning what God is doing and trying hard not to get in God's way. Listening, recognizing the changes that are taking place, and affirming the experience are all important. Listening shows that you take the person and his or her experience seriously. It's true and it matters. Here the director's discernment is very important in recognizing the signs of the beginning of contemplative prayer. There are not so many techniques to teach; it's much more a question of encouraging an attitude of quiet availability, of a gentle continuous desire to be there for God in the silence, of being kind and gentle with yourself, rather than being anxious to achieve success in prayer.

I have found it helpful to think of spiritual muscles. In an earlier time, when prayer was active, people used the muscles of concentration, feelings, imagination, thinking and words. Now none of these seem to do any good. In fact, trying to use them gets in the way. Now that their prayer has become passive there are other muscles to develop, such as relaxation, openness and simply being aware.

I'm sure that I am not alone in finding that certain words and ideas repeat themselves with a growing emphasis in my meetings with different men and women. A couple of years ago I found that the words that kept coming to me as I sat with people were 'gift' and 'grace'. All this prayer is gift from God. Our natural attitude is thanking. Then recently another word has arrived. It is 'achievement'. If it is all gift and grace, then why are we trying so hard to achieve it for ourselves? Achievement is about my success, about my effort getting me there, while all the time contemplative prayer is about God's work and my simply being open to that, letting the self-centred striving fall away. It is not so much a matter of trying to love God, as simply letting God love you.

Although most people are brought up in an active style of praying, I have found that those who come from an evangelical background have their own particular problems in the transition toward silent prayer. One of the gifts of that tradition is the strong commitment to being an active Christian in response to the experience of conversion. Active in evangelism and service, their prayer is often also very active and disciplined, based on study of the Bible and expressed in words. The move toward silence can cause a deep conflict with such a person's past awareness of duty to God. He or she may also face incomprehension or even hostility from others within their church. There is work to be done in direction in listening, discerning and affirming the path on which someone is being led.

Distractions

Angus J. Kennedy, in *The Internet Rough Guide 2000*, wrote:

If you start receiving piles of unsolicited mail (commonly known as spam) contrary to popular advice, there's not a lot you can do about it. You can employ various filters, but there's really not much point. You might as well let them arrive and delete them on sight.

Let the parable, like all good parables, do its own work for you!

Distractions in prayer must be the most usual problem that people bring. However, rather than the distractions themselves, it is getting upset and guilty over them that really hinders prayer. Wandering thoughts and explosive feelings are going to happen. People need to be encouraged to return over and over again to the real business of the prayer. As in the whole of contemplative praying, it is a matter of focus. If you beat yourself up because you are faced with distractions and you can't control them, if you get upset and condemn yourself as a failure, then your focus is on yourself and you are making yourself responsible for the 'success' of your prayer. The contemplative's true focus can only be on God, who gives the prayer in the first place. The director's job is to help people to be gentle with themselves, to recognize that the human mind is designed to work in such a way that distractions will happen and to move away from them back to God. You may want to follow the advice given in *The Cloud of Unknowing* about returning to the 'sacred word' as a sign of our willingness to be there available to God, or you may want to use a mantra or an awareness of your breathing – whatever you use, all these techniques are all designed to help you to let go of that focus on yourself and place your willing attention back on God. Simply to let yourself be loved by God.

St Teresa of Avila has a lovely image of working in the convent garden and letting the flies buzz around her head while she concentrates on the real business of hoeing.

Among the most seductive thoughts are the holy ones. You find you are writing sermons to yourself or for other people, thinking about how to express your belief, or doing a kind of self-assessment on how well (or how badly) you are praying.

Helps

Contemplative prayer is quite a lonely road to travel. Particularly in the drier desert stretches it is good to have company. That is why it is important to have a sensitive director, someone who can offer some discernment and reassurance. But other companions are important too. Recently I have offered those whom I direct the opportunity to meet twice a year for a short retreat of 48 hours. We alternate times of prayer with review sessions, opportunities for fellowship and plenty of rest. It is remarkable how being in prayer together with other people can help to deepen awareness, and how encouraging it is to hear other people describing the ordinariness of their way of praying!

With the way of contemplation there can be a danger of imbalance. Spiritual feet need to be kept firmly on the ground by regular liturgical prayer and a continuing sacramental life, together with the meditative use of the

Bible provided in *lectio divina*. It may be a lonely calling, but it helps to remember that the people who undertake it are members of the body of Christ and have their fellowship with others in him.

What follows?

People rightly ask their director what they might expect as they develop in this way. And the simple answer is that nobody knows. It may be that they are led deeper and deeper along the road that leads to mystical union with a spiritual awareness that gives them great joy. It may be that their road follows that path that St John of the Cross gave as the route to Mount Carmel, when he described it as *nada*, simply nothing.

What seems to be certain is that the spiritual excitements, even the insights and assurances, are only accompaniments to prayer, not prayer itself. Indeed they need to be treated almost as distractions from the true path of the prayer. Awareness of God's closeness or presence, feelings of sexual arousal, a sense of overwhelming awe or of one's own littleness in the face of such love – these are not the heart of contemplative prayer. They need to be talked about in direction, certainly, and their value carefully weighed, but if they are given too much weight, they are in danger of becoming ends in themselves.

What is quite clear both from the long and deep Christian tradition and from contemporary experience is that the contemplative way is a reminder that prayer is a gift from God and that its end is in God.

Resources

As will have become obvious throughout the book, the main resources for spiritual direction are to be found within the people concerned and in God's grace present and active in their meeting. This is not to say that training for directors is unnecessary; there is much to be learned from the reading, teaching and supervised practice to be found in the courses that are on offer.

The work of a director can from time to time be demanding, occasionally painful and sometimes draining. When it is working well the ministry is to some extent its own resource. There is a mutuality and a balance. But the weight of accompanying someone in distress or facing difficult problems can drain a director's resources. 'He ain't heavy. He's my brother' is a good, strong song and it carries a certain truth. But directors need to make sure that their own resources are cared for. Their own practice of prayer is central. It is also valuable to have some sort of supervision in which they can talk openly about the effect that directing is having on them and in that way ease the pressure. It can be either in a small group or one-to-one with an individual supervisor. This supervision is not concerned with asking for advice about the people who come for help and the problems they pose, because confidentiality precludes that. It is there to help directors deal with the reactions, the feeling and the spiritual effects that their ministry produces in them.

Tools

Many directors find that, when they meet with new people and also as they accompany men and women on their continuing journey, it is helpful to have in mind some kind of filter or matrix with which to sort the information they are receiving. There are at least two kinds of these tools. One is concerned with the sort of personality a person has and the other is concerned with the stage of spiritual or religious development at which that person finds himself or herself. By using these tools sensitively, directors can recognize for themselves attitudes and ways of behaviour in people and can help them to recognize that their personality and interests are not abnormal, but conform to a natural way for people to live.

Myers–Briggs
The Myers–Briggs Personality Type Indicator has in some quarters almost come to be regarded as a vital part of the director's equipment. Working from Jung's analysis of personalities, Isabel Myers and her mother Katharine Briggs developed in the 1950s their own way of identify-ing 16 different patterns of people's preferred way of behaviour. The language of the eight initial letters has become very useful jargon in the world of pastoral care.

The four pairs of preferences are about positions on a scale between opposing poles. 'E' and 'I' stand for 'Extrovert' and 'Introvert', with the words used in their generally accepted sense. 'N' and 'S' stand for 'Intuition' and 'Sensation'. The S person tends to work in the area of facts, of past experience. The N person is alive to metaphor and imagery and to what might happen in the future. Jung classified people who choose an impersonal basis for choice as 'Thinking' ('T') people and those who choose a personal basis as 'Feeling' ('F') people. T people are more comfortable with objective judgements. F people feel more comfortable with value judgements. The final pair is the scale between 'J' and 'P', 'Judging' and 'Perceiving'. J people prefer things to be settled; P people keep options open and fluid. A J person tries to get things done by the deadline that has been set. For P people, deadlines are interesting phenomena that do not really impinge on their lives.

By using a carefully constructed questionnaire it is possible to recognize where someone's preferred pattern of behaviour lies on these four scales and to recognize traits in that person's personality that are shared by others who are in a similar place. Shorthand use of the letters gives a language in which to talk about people's preferred attitudes and ways of acting. An INFJ person, for instance, will be recognizably different from an ESTP person.

This indicator is very useful in creating a kind of geography by which to understand the human landscape. It has the real gift of helping people to recognize and value their own nature. It enables them to see that the way they are is a natural and genuine way of being human, rather than being different from other people and therefore wrong. It can enlighten and affirm. For example, in a busy, achievement-oriented society, notice how many people apologize for being introverts.

It is not only where people are strong that is important. As well as noting their preferred way of behaviour Myers–Briggs also shows what Jung called their 'shadow' – that part of a person's temperament that lies fallow or hidden and yet is there to be recognized and helped to grow. This recognition may be of great value in spiritual direction.

With all its positive aspects it has to be recognized that the Myers–Briggs Personality Type Indicator can be open to misuse. When it is taken to be prescriptive rather than descriptive it can lead to all sorts of trouble. Kenneth Leech underlines this danger when he refers to Myers–Briggs as 'astrology for the middle classes'. When behaviour is excused on the grounds that it is the only the outworking of some kind of destiny, there is a distortion of the truth. To say that you are of a certain type does not relieve you from the responsibility of making your own decisions, nor on the other hand does it mean that you have to behave in a way that is expected from people of that type.

The enneagram

The origins of the enneagram are shrouded in the mists of history. In itself it is a figure of a nine-pointed star enclosed in a circle. Used as a diagram for describing types of people with different sorts of personalities it has found wide acceptance in many parts of the Church. It would seem that its roots may lie in the Sufi tradition of Islamic spirituality. First introduced into the West by G. I. Gurdjieff as he fled the Russian revolution to find refuge in France, it was developed by his followers and in particular by P. D. Ouspensky. In the 1970s Oscar Ichazo, a Bolivian, offered the symbol as a paradigm for understanding different aspects of human nature and through his work in New York it became known in the USA. Since then there has been a growing use of the approach in the churches, developed with Christian insights as a way of identifying nine particular types of personality.

The nine types, known simply by their number, can be described by identifying specific compulsions that belong to each group of people. These are a response to particular fears that come from life's earliest experience and lead a person to develop distinctive ways of avoidance that shape his or her preferred attitudes. So, to outline it very shortly: ONEs avoid anger and strive for perfection in what they do; TWOs avoid recognizing that they have needs and make a point of being helpful to others; THREEs avoid failure and work hard for success in their life; FOURs avoid ordinariness by seeing themselves as being special; FIVEs avoid emptiness and try to amass knowledge; SIXes avoid deviance and are firmly tied to regulations; SEVENs avoid pain and exhibit strong optimism and enjoyment; EIGHTs avoid weakness and take pride in being strong people; and NINEs avoid conflict and are concerned for peace, both within themselves and among those with whom they are in contact.

A further grouping can be made according to the preferred centres that people use for functioning with conscious energy. These are the gut centre, which draws on instincts and habits; the heart centre, with its feelings and emotions; and the head centre, strong on thinking and reflection. Grouped under the gut centre are numbers one, eight and nine; the heart takes numbers two, three and four; and the head numbers five, six and seven.

As with the Myers–Briggs Personality Type Indicator, it is impossible to present with any fairness a way of understanding and relating with people that needs time and dialogue to enter into. The importance of the enneagram as a possible tool for the work of spiritual direction in accompanying personal change and development lies in its strength not only as a way into self-knowledge, but also as a means of fostering transformation or conversion.

There is a very large provision of books about these two popular ways of categorizing personalities – Myers–Briggs and the enneagram – and it is possible to understand something of their methods by reading. For example, I have found *Please Understand Me: Character and Temperament Type* by David Keirsey and Marilyn Bates a good, practical introduction to Myers–Briggs, and Bruce Duncan's *Pray Your Way: Your Personality and God* to be helpful in relating the categories to spirituality. Among a vast array of writings on the enneagram I chose *The Enneagram and Spiritual Direction: Nine Paths to Spiritual Guidance*, in which James Empereur applies his understanding of the enneagram to his experience of spiritual direction. However, by far the best way to enter into the basic theory and the practical working of these two disciplines is to join a course or a workshop and learn by personal experience of the method with an experienced teacher.

Stages of faith

For centuries spiritual teachers have realized that people tend to develop along recognizable lines and pass through recognizable stages. In their own different ways St Teresa of Avila, St John of the Cross and St Ignatius Loyola, to name but a few examples of influential writers, all recognized that people needed to arrive at a certain level of spiritual development before they could move on to the next. Since the work of James Fowler with his books such as *Stages of Faith* and *Becoming Adult, Becoming Christian*, it has become usual to note that people can be at many different points along a range of ways of believing and of relating to faith and a faith community. Fowler proposes a series of seven stages of development along the way of maturity. Using somewhat obscure academic language, he names them 'primal faith', 'intuitive–projective faith, 'mythic–literal faith', 'synthetic–conventional faith', 'individuative–reflective faith', 'conjunctive faith' and 'universalizing faith'.

Elizabeth Liebert proposes just three stages of changing patterns of attitude and behaviour in her *Changing Life Patterns: Adult Development in Spiritual Direction*. Her 'conformist stage', 'conscientious stage' and 'interindividual stage' relate quite closely to the three aspects of religion and religious people noted by von Hügel when he wrote about the different *attraits* as the 'institutional', the 'intellectual' and the 'mystical'. She points out that people in the first stage are less likely to seek to be accompanied in spiritual direction than those who are more open in the second.

Books

Rather than list the wide and deep resource that lies in books about the Christian journey and spiritual direction, I simply note a number that I have personally found helpful. This is always dangerous. Different books appeal to different people, and another person's recommendation may not appeal. Equally, a book may leave you cold one year and some years later may speak to you directly. So with that provisos, I offer my selection.

On the main topic of spiritual direction, I suggest Kenneth Leech's *Soul Friend: A Study in Spirituality* as a book that has been very important in the development of the ministry and gives a fine overview. Margaret Guenther, an Episcopal priest in the USA, writes from long experience both as a director and as a teacher in the field of spirituality in her *Holy Listening: The Art of Spiritual Direction*. Gordon Jeff led one of the earliest training courses, SPI-DIR, in the Southwark diocese. His *Spiritual Direction for Every Christian* draws on his time there. There are many other books on the shelves in church book shops, mostly from the USA. Many of them deal with spiritual direction for particular groups of people.

On prayer there is a vast range of titles with authors from virtually every Christian century. Here especially, one needs to be aware of choosing the right book that will meet individual needs or that suits the present situation. Some books give a general survey of different ways of prayer; among them I suggest Richard Foster's *Prayer: Finding the Heart's True Home* as being particularly useful. Foster is an American Quaker who writes positively about a comprehensive selection of prayer methods from the classical schools of prayer to some of its more extreme contemporary manifestations. Moving on to consider books on the contemplative prayer of silence, I have been greatly helped by the writing of Robert Llewelyn. His *With Pity Not With Blame* presents the story and teaching of Julian of Norwich and the insights of the anonymous author of *The Cloud of Unknowing*. Llewelyn's *Thirsting for God* collects together addresses on key scriptural topics that he gave when he was chaplain to the Sisters of the Love of God at Bede House in Kent. I also owe much to the work of Thomas Keating and his writing, beginning with *Open Mind, Open Heart*.

Among editions of classic texts and introductory books, I have appreciated William Johnston's edition of *The Cloud of Unknowing*. Johnston has also written *Being in Love* as notes about the art of prayer to 'Thomas', someone responsible for a spiritual centre. It is full of perceptive and practical advice. Eileen Lyddon's *Door Through Darkness* is an accessible introduction to the work of St John of the Cross.

Books are a help, certainly. They can inspire, encourage and give new insights, but they can never be substitutes for the real thing, which is doing it yourself!

In conclusion

At the close of this book there are two strands that call for comment. There is a note on what it may mean for individuals and there is a note on questions that the practice of spiritual direction poses about the church.

The process by which this book came to be written, growing out of a series of conversations between an author and about 30 people, has delivered a wide and rich input of experience and comment from a group of both men and women, some ordained and some lay, a few of whom also work as directors. My hope is that readers seeking to learn more about the practice and the potential of spiritual direction will have recognized at least some things in the accounts of these people that reflect their own story or echo their own requirements. But certainly not everything will have been relevant to everyone. We are each separate people with our own individuality.

The purpose has been to demonstrate how the relationship and the regular meetings of spiritual direction offer anyone who desires to go down that road an accompanied journey in faith. Both during those meetings and before and after them there is the opportunity to reflect on one's own life and all that it contains in the light of the gospel with a companion in a special, privileged sort of friendship. In direction there is space to hear what the word of faith has say to inform one's choices, one's attitudes and one's judgements.

There are common threads running through all of the stories and opinions referred to here, but it needs to be remembered that, however much similarity there is, no one person's story is going to be the same as anyone else's. There are no universally applicable patterns for the journey of faith. We are all individuals and follow our own individual ways. However, I hope that what is written here may have given readers enough evidence to decide whether or not spiritual direction would be right for them.

Turning to look at the relationship between direction and the church, one observation stands out. It is that, to judge from the quotations from people, the work done in direction fills a recognizable gap in what is on offer from many local churches. People very frequently come to direction because they are aware of changes in their life, or because they sense that they are being invited to grow and develop as Christian men or women. But in only a few neighbourhood churches is the development of individual members towards Christian maturity publicly recognized as a priority or catered for in the regular life of the congregation. The increasing popularity of spiritual direction can be seen either as a source of help that makes up for a lack in the mainstream Church or as a challenge to the leadership in local communities to be more aware of the often unspoken need for that help. So spiritual direction can be regarded by some people involved in it as, in a sense, an alternative to the formal church.

On the other hand, my own experience of working as a director convinces me that spiritual direction is, by its very nature, a ministry of the church. It may not be an official ministry in the sense of being licensed by ecclesiastical authority or having a place in any official liturgy, but it has its proper place within the community in obedience to the injunctions to love one's neighbour and to bear one another's burdens. Spiritual direction and its growth in many different parts of the Christian Church is surely a sign that the Holy Spirit is active in renewing the people of God for witness, mission and service in the world.